THE BOOK OF ALLISON
the wounds you don't see

ALLISON K. JAMES-FRISON

&

Nicole K. Horn-Shelton

Contributed to Chapter Two and Three

Copyright ©2025 by Allison K. James-Frison

All rights reserved. No part of this book may be reproduced, copied, stored, or transmitted in any form or by any means- graphic, electronic, or mechanical, including photocopying, recording, scanning, or information storage and retrieval systems without the prior permission of Allison K. James-Frison except were permitted by law.

Published by: Allison K. James-Frison

Written by: Allison K. James – Frison

ISBN Paperback: 979-8-218-82070-1

ISBN eBook: B0GCC5T2YQ (Amazon)

Cover Design by Danielle Moore

Printed in the United States of America

For more information, visit:

Website: Www.TheBookOfAllison.com

For Speaking Events, Meet and Greets or Book Singing

Email address: TheBookofAllison@gmail.com

Follow Allison on Social Media:

Facebook: Author Allison K. James – Frison

Instagram: TheBookofAllison_

DEDICATION

This book is dedicated to those who have faced adversity, endured hardships, suffered in silence—and still found the strength to rise again. Life's challenges, whether in the form of personal loss, trauma, or unexpected obstacles—do not define us. It is how we respond that shapes our path forward.

To the ones who have been told "you can't" and chose to believe "I still will," this is for you. May these pages remind you that your story is not over, your voice matters, and your journey has purpose. You are living proof that brokenness can give birth to brilliance, and healing is possible—even after the deepest wounds.

To the loving memory of my parents, Spencer L. James, Sr., and Zanna E. Hadley-James—although you were called home to be with the Lord at an early age, I know you are watching over your children. You both taught me invaluable lessons about resilience, faith, sacrifice, and unconditional love. The foundation you laid has carried me through life's most difficult seasons, and I feel your presence with me every step of the way.

Your wisdom, your strength, and your prayers are the roots from which I continue to grow. I have passed your values on to my daughter, your granddaughter and to the many young people I mentored—ensuring that your legacy continues to light the path for generations to come.

To my siblings we made it through the storms. I thank God for you all, you all paid a special part of my life regardless of what life may have taken us through we made it together, I love you all with all my heart. We are Spencer and Zanna's children. Let's not forget where our legacy started.

To my Aunties, Fannie, Ina, Mattie, and Uncle Olan (Balow): I love you all so much. When my father passed away it was his sisters and brother that made sure, we had everything that we needed. You all treated my mother like she was your biological sister and took care of all of her eight children. I cannot express the amount of love and gratefulness I have for you all. Grandma Carrie Mae James and your brother Spencer L. James, Sr., would be so proud of you.

To my community sisters and friends who continue to cheer and clap for me in rooms that I am not in and support me during some of the most challenging times of my life. I wish I could name you all; however, I do want to leave anyone out just know that I appreciate and love you all.

ACKNOWLEDGMENT

To my amazing and supportive husband, Andre Frison — Poppa Bear — it has been one of life's greatest blessings to live, love, and laugh with you. You walked into my heart and brought peace where there was chaos, light where there was darkness, and joy where there was silence. Your unwavering love, patience, and quiet strength have carried me through more than you know. Thank you for being my silent hero, my protector, my best friend, and the anchor that keeps me grounded. I thank God for you daily.

To my darling daughter, Rashanna — The Black Unicorn — A Daughter from Newark you are my heart in human form. You made my life complete in ways I never thought possible. Watching you blossom into the intelligent, courageous, and purpose-driven young woman you are today has been the greatest honor of my life. Mommy is beyond proud of you. Continue to walk boldly in your God-given purpose, knowing that you were born to stand out, to lead, and to shine. Never shrink to fit in— your magic was made to be seen.

To my siblings, thank you for walking this journey with me through all its heights and lows. We have faced our share of storms, but we have held on to each other through it all. Our bond is unbreakable, our love unconditional, and our strength generational. We will continue to stand united, lift each other up when we fall, and carry the torch of our family's legacy. We made it. I love you all deeply. RIP Spencer L. James, Jr. your memory lives on in every step we take.

And to everyone who has ever spoken a kind word, offered a prayer, or held space for my healing—thank you. This book reflects your love, your impact, and your presence in my life.

To Nicole K. Horn-Shelton, thank you for believing in me, my story, and my vision. Your support in this process was appreciated. Authornicolehornshelton@gmail.com

To my therapist — thank you for helping me peel back the layers, confront the wounds, and giving me the courage to rewrite the narrative of my life with truth, compassion, and strength. It is a joy to have you on my team.

Kadian Peynado

Epiphany Relationship and Family Counseling, LLC

Website: www.epiphrfc.com

Email: Epiphrfc@gmail.com

Phone Number: 908-531-6905

PREFACE

There are wounds that leave scars you can see—and there are wounds that never show, yet shape everything you become. The Book of Allison: The Wounds You Don't See was born from the latter.

For years, I carried unspoken pain behind my smile, hidden inside my strength, and disguised in the roles I played—wife, mother, leader, deaconess, survivor, servant. I appeared whole while quietly breaking in places no one could see. Healing, I learned, begins not with silence, but with acknowledgment.

This book comes from the messy middle of becoming, not from the mountaintop of victory. These pages reveal trauma, betrayal, lessons, rebuilding, and the awakening of my voice. I chose transparency over perfection, because someone out there needs the chapter I once could not find.

This is more than my story, it's a mirror. Your unseen wounds do not disqualify you from healing, joy, or purpose. My hope is that these pages help you feel seen, strengthened, and empowered to continue your journey toward healing.

DISCLAIMER

This book shares my personal experiences, reflections, and lessons learned on the journey of healing from trauma. Some topics may be sensitive or difficult to read. This book is meant to inspire, support, and offer insight, but it is not a substitute for professional advice, therapy, or medical care.

If you are experiencing distress or emotional challenges, I encourage you to reach out to a qualified mental health professional or trusted support system. While I share my story with honesty and heart, the author and publisher cannot be held responsible for individual outcomes. By reading, you acknowledge that this book is intended to offer guidance, hope, and encouragement, not professional treatment.

I, Allison James – Frison do not intend to harm, defame, or cause distress to any person, living or deceased. Any resemblance to actual persons or events outside of my own life, is either coincidental or has been fictionalized for narrative clarity.

With truth and courage,

Author Allison K. James-Frison

Introduction

Dear Reader,

As you open this book, I want you to know something important: I understand. I understand what it feels like to carry pain silently, to wonder if anyone will ever see the real you, and to question if life will ever feel gentle again. I have walked through storms that felt endless, and I have stumbled more times than I can count.

But I am here to tell you something I learned along the way: you are not broken beyond repair. You are not defined by the moments that hurt you or the people who failed to see your worth. There is a light inside you, even if it flickers sometimes, even if the world has tried to dim it. And that light—your light—can guide you through the darkest nights.

This book is my story, yes, but it is also an invitation. An invitation to walk with me through the challenges, the heartbreak, and the victories. It is meant to remind you that healing is possible, that second chances exist, and that your voice—no matter how quiet it feels right now—matters.

Along the way, you will read about moments that broke me, but also moments that rebuilt me. You will see that life is not about perfection or having all the answers—it is about resilience, courage, and the small choices that push us forward when hope seems distant.

I share this with you because I believe in the power of connection. I believe that our stories, when shared, can heal, inspire, and empower one another. I want you to know that you are not alone in your struggles, and that even the wounds you carry can become the source of strength for yourself and for others.

So, as you turn the pages, I invite you to breathe, to reflect, and to believe in the possibility of hope. Your journey matters, your story matters, and the best chapters of your life are still waiting to be written.

With all my heart,

Author Allison K. James – Frison

CONTENTS

ONE
FAMILY THE PEOPLE WHO KNEW ME FIRST..............1
WORKBOOK: THE FOUNDATION WE STOOD ON..........28

TWO
EVERY APOLOGY CAME WITH A SCAR.......................30
WORKBOOK: DOMESTIC VIOLENCE...............................51

THREE
EVERYTHING I OWNED IN A BAG..................................53
WORKBOOK: HOMELESSNESS..60

FOUR
SURVIVING THE TRIGGER...62
WORKBOOK: GUN VIOLENCE...77

FIVE
BREAKING THE SILENCE...80
WORKBOOK: TRAUMA & CHILD ABUSE.......................88

SIX
I'M STILL SMART I JUST LEARN DIFFERENTLY.......91
WORKBOOK: EDUCATION AND POLITICS......................94

SEVEN
THE VOICES OF GIRLS MATTER..................................97
WORKBOOK: IDENTITY AND SELF-WORTH.................100

EIGHT
DAUGHTER: THE WORLD WILL CALL HER MANY THINGS...115
WORKBOOK: A DAUGHTER FROM NEWARK...............122

NINE
CALL TO SERVE...126
WORKBOOK: KNOW YOUR CALLING............................129

TEN
WHEN THE DUST CLEARED..138
WORKBOOK: SECOND CHANCE.......................................148

ELEVEN
SPIRITUAL ENCOUNTERS...155
WORKBOOK: SPIRITUAL ENCOUNTERS.......................164

The Book of Allison: The Wounds You Don't See

Chapter 1

Written By Allison K. James – Frison

Family: The People Who Knew Me First

FAMILY – The word "family" holds deep meaning for me because I loved my parents and siblings dearly. My parents were the glue that kept us together when life tried to pull us apart. My dad always told me I would be the one to change the world, but I know that change begins at home.

If I cannot pour love, forgiveness, and strength into my own family, how can I expect to carry it into the world? It saddens me when family members lean on outsiders more than their own blood. However, this has never been the case for me.

Family should be the first place we run to, not the last. Of course, we will disagree, and yes, we may even hurt one another with words or actions, but I refuse to let that be the reason for separation. We must break the generational curses that have lingered far too long. Cycles of silence, pride, resentment, and pain must stop with us.

Love must take the front seat, guiding our decisions and softening our hearts. Because in the end, when all else fades, it is family who remains. And if I can heal there first, I can then heal the world around me. My father, Spencer James Sr., was born in Phoenix City, Alabama, and my mother, Zanna E. Hadley-James, was born in Columbus, Georgia. As an inquisitive child, I loved listening to stories from their past.

I remember hearing my mom and my maternal auntie talk about their teenage years when they used to cross the river to Phoenix City, AL to meet the boys. I am fairly sure they were sneaking across the river. I bet that is how my parents met, and our family started ending up with eight children.

My father left Alabama when he was a teenager. He hitchhiked his way to New Jersey. My mom was pregnant, so he decided to leave her behind but promised to send for her once he settled. He did, and that is how our family established a life in Newark, New Jersey.

The Book of Allison: The Wounds You Don't See

Momma: Ms. Zanna James: Discipline Wrapped in Love

My mom ruled with an iron fist she demanded structure and obedience. Our household consisted of both my parents and seven siblings, two brothers, five sisters, and me, which could get pretty hectic at times. We were raised in a strict household with many rules. Immediately after school, we had to take off our school clothes, do our homework, eat, and then we were allowed to go outside—but only for a brief time. As soon as the streetlights came on, we had to be back inside. My mom would stick her head out of her bedroom window and call us one by one until we were all in the house and accounted for.

The other kids in the neighborhood would tease us because we had to go inside when the streetlights came on or because we could not leave from in front the building without our mom knowing where we were going. If we did leave, at least two of us had to go together, no matter where we were headed. We had set times for everything: set mealtimes, set wake-up times for school, set bedtimes, and, of course, "I'm going to whip your ass" time. The weekend was clean the house day from front to back even if the house was not dirty, we still had to clean up. I remember watching my mother rip paper up and toss them around the floor because my siblings and, I would say "mom the house is not dirty."

As a child, I thought this was extreme. But as an adult and a parent, I have come to realize that this was love, structure, and discipline. My father showed his affection differently than my mother. My mother was the disciplinarian, but they shared one common value: education. They did not play about our academics. We were never allowed to miss school. We went to school in the rain, sleet, and snowstorms. Education was key in our household, and it was non-negotiable.

My mother became ill when I was a young girl. I remember her constantly going in and out of the hospital, undergoing multiple surgeries. At the time, I did not understand the nature of her illness, although I am sure my older siblings were more aware of her diagnosis. What I do remember vividly is watching her give herself injections—what I now know was insulin. I later learned she had diabetes, a disease that slowly took a toll on her body over time and eventually led to her needing weekly dialysis treatments. Watching her fight through it all left a lasting impact on me, even at such an early age.

At one point, we all played a role in being her caregivers. Looking back, I do not think we fully understood that we were caregivers at the time. We were just doing what any child would do for their mother. Despite her illness, her commitment to us never wavered. She was always present in our lives. My mom never missed any back-to-school nights, parent-teacher conferences, graduations, award ceremonies, or proms and there were plenty. She was fully engaged with all eight of her children, even though she was battling her own health issues.

Not only was my mom present in our lives, but she was also a community mom. She took care of everyone. If someone needed a place to stay, my mom would let them sleep on the sofa. She would take food from our cabinets and fridge to give to neighbors and families who needed it more than we did. The mothers in the projects helped one another. I recall her sending letters to her friends, asking if she could borrow fifty dollars until her welfare check came in. They borrowed everything from one another—bread, eggs, flour, canned milk, sugar, and butter were the most common items. Even during holidays like the Fourth of July and Labor Day, my mom would buy one hundred hot dogs, hamburgers, rolls and buns. I never understood why she would buy so much food when she only had eight children.

The Book of Allison: The Wounds You Don't See

As I got older, I realized she was not just feeding her children; she was feeding the children in the community. During the summer, she would buy fifty popsicles from the ice cream truck and break them in half so one hundred kids could enjoy a cool treat on a sweltering day. If she could not afford popsicles, she would make homemade ones from Kool-Aid.

She would fill ice trays with Kool-Aid, stick popsicle sticks in, and freeze them. When the ice cream truck arrived, she would send one of her children upstairs to grab the frozen Kool-Aid treats from the freezer.

My mom did not stop there. She was also a volunteer parent at Quitman Street School in Newark. She would bring extra ribbons, barrettes, socks, hair grease, combs, and brushes to help fix the hair of kids who were unkempt and Vaseline when faces were ashy every child had a shiny face under her watch. Years later, I ran into people who still remember my mom and told me how much they loved her.

My mom was not just a strict disciplinarian; she gave authority to all the parents in our building to discipline her children. If we disrespected anyone, or if she was told that we disrespected anyone in authority, we got a whooping.

The adults in the neighborhood acted like the neighborhood watch committee, and the neighborhood watch committee did not play around they carried a belt with them waiting to catch someone misbehaving.

I can remember muffled laughs and tiptoeing as we tried sneaking out when mom fell asleep. But as soon as we tried sneaking back in, she was always there, sitting at the front door with her belt ready to give us a slap with the belt on our butts. At least the party was fun while it lasted. I swear we were doing the WOP while getting our butts whipped.

One time, I tried sneaking in after curfew. When I opened the door, my mom was standing there with the belt. I tried to run, but she grabbed me. In the struggle, I pulled away, ripping my shirt from her grasp. I decided to run away because I did not want to face the consequences, but I had nowhere to go.

I spent hours running up and down the stairs from the first to the 12th floor until I was hungry and needed the bathroom. I thought she would have let me slide because of how frightened I was, but no, she still whipped me, I was so mad and said to myself "I should have stayed in the hallway overnight." I did the most when it was time for me to get a whipping I rolled on the floor, jumped up and down like I was jumping rope; however, it did not matter mom always caught me in the middle of moving around and the belt always landed on my butt.

Mom didn't always whip us, she was caring, loving, and gentle. She always made a way out of no way when it came to her children. She sacrificed everything for us.

The Book of Allison: The Wounds You Don't See

Daddy: Spencer L. James, Sr: The Shepherd of Our Home

I had an amazing relationship with my father. He believed in me and saw something special in me from an early age. In my mind, I was his favorite. He never called me Allison. He had nicknames for me, like "Princess" and "Al-Duke." He always said I was the one who would change the world. I did not know Duke meant "leader" at the time, but whenever his friends visited, he would call me in the living room and say, "This is my princess, she's the one who's going to change the world."

Mom and Dad had a loving relationship for many years. They never had a physical fight that I knew of. My mom was adamant that my dad could not drink in the house, so he would usually come home intoxicated. For whatever reason, he would take us to the bar every Easter. I do not know what kind of tradition this was, but as kids, we were excited to be there.

He would sit us at the back of the bar, and the bartender would give us cookies and milk. No one was allowed to talk to us, or they would see my dad's alter ego, "DOC," emerge.

He carried a stick and called it the 'Be Cool Stick.' If anyone disrespected him or his family, they would get the DOC treatment and end up in the emergency room.

My dad's drinking may have been part of the reason my parents separated when I was five. However, they never got a divorce. At first, I was unaware that they were separated. I was still seeing my dad every day.

It was not until I was about ten that I realized my dad was not coming home for good, and I figured this out by eavesdropping. It was the small things that I missed the most about my father.

The smell of his shaving cream, watching him crack eggs in a glass with milk, pepper and drink the eggs straight out of the glass, watching him love all over my mother and, placing money on the kitchen table when he got paid for my mother to take care of the children. I missed running to him whenever he walked into the door screaming "daddies home." Those memories will never leave me.

My older sibling would tell us stories about how my father would gather them around the bed and pray over his wife and children. I was not part of that tradition; however, I wish I had experienced those moments. He was a sharp dresser; his hats and shades game was on point. My daddy could not do anything wrong in my eyes.

Unfortunately, both my parents are resting in divine peace. I was seventeen when my father was a victim of a violent crime, I had just graduated out of high school – seventeen years old, with plans to attend college; however, when my father died my self-esteem died with him.

Nobody was telling me I was the one anymore, beautiful, smart or, any of the adjustives that my father used to call me. I was afraid to leave home, the projects where I felt safe. My mother died of a heart attack while at dialysis, I was just becoming a woman at the age of twenty-four years old. I miss them deeply.

A Brother's Love: I Call Him Orlandrus: The Oldest Out of Eight Children.

Some boys grow up with the freedom to just be children. They run the streets with their friends, laugh without worry, and think only about themselves. But for Orlandus, childhood ended the moment responsibility knocked on our door. When our mother grew sick and our parents separated, the weight of the household fell squarely on his young shoulders and my oldest sister Shelva.

He was still just a teenager, yet he carried himself like a man twice his age. While others his age were chasing after fun and freedom, Orlandus was learning the language of sacrifice. He made sure food was in the kitchen, bills were paid on time, and that the household kept running even when life tried to tear it apart. To me, he was not just a brother, he was a provider and a steady force when everything else felt uncertain.

The way Orlandus loved us was not loud or showy. His love spoke in action. It spoke in the quiet moments when he came home with groceries after working long hours. It spoke in a careful way he managed bills at the kitchen table and refused to let us go without. It spoke every time we reached out for him, and he showed up—without hesitation, without excuses.

When our parents went their separate ways, Orlandus stepped into the gap that was left behind. Not because he wanted to, but because love demanded it.

He became the head of the household before he was even grown, making sure we felt safe, covered, and cared for. He did not just keep the house together—he kept us together.

And then came the darkest moment of all. Losing our father had already carved a wound in us, one we carried every day.

But five years later, when our mother passed away, the bottom seemed to fall out of our world. Eight children left without parents. The weight of grief was crushing, and the uncertainty of what would come next was almost unbearable.

I remember the night so clearly. The house was heavy with silence, each of us lost in our own pain. That is when Orlandus gathered all of us together at our mother's apartment. His voice was steady; his eyes filled with both sorrow and strength.

He told us everything was going to be all right, that we were going to get through this—not alone, but as a family. And somehow, in that moment, I believed him. I believed it because he had always treated us like we were his children. He had already proven, repeatedly, that he would not let us fall apart.

Orlandus could have walked away. The weight was far greater than any young man should have had to carry. Eight children without parents were a challenge that could have broken anyone.

But instead of running, he chose to rise. He continued to raise us up, stepping fully into a role he was never asked to fill but one he embraced with love and loyalty.

Looking back, I see now that his sacrifices were not just duty, they were devotion. He did not just step in where our parents could not; he embodied what it truly means to stand in the gap for family. His choices, his sacrifices, his presence shaped us more than I understood at the time.

Orlandus became the soft hero of our story. The one who bore the weight without complaint, who gave without asking for anything in return, who showed us what unconditional love looks like when it has lived out every single day.

However, when we were younger and we got on his nerve or misbehaved the knuckle sandwich came out, he would ball his index finger up and knock us upside the head, I sure do not miss those knuckle sandwiches. When I tried to run from him, I would take fourteen steps and he would only take two steps; he was seven feet tall, and his two steps were more powerful than my fourteen steps. The grabbing of my shirt collar was funny and scary.

Even now, that bond is unshakable. Because when life pressed down on us, Orlandus rose. When storms raged around us, he stood tall, shielding us from the worst of it. And when we called—whether out of need, fear, or longing—he always answered. Always.

When it was time for me to get married, he stepped in and gave me away to my husband at my wedding, he danced with me during the father – daughter danced. He made sure I had something old, new, and blue. He gave me my mother's diamond pearl ring inside of a gold and blue case; I could not believe it. I told him I wanted a "Royal Wedding" he made his own King's outfit and crowned me on my wedding day.

When he built his house, he built it with his siblings in mind when we go visit. We all have our own rooms; he cooks for us like we are children and continues to make sure that we stay together.

That is a brother's love. That is Orlandus. As adults his six sisters still call on him to keep us together. I know I tell him all the time; however, I love you with all my heart and soul you are the true meaning of a brother's love.

My Second Mom Shelva Is Her Name: The Oldest Out of Six Sisters.

Every family has that one sibling who somehow feels more like a parent than a sister. For us, that was Shelva. She was not just our big sister—she was our second mom.

Shelva often said she wished she had a big sister to guide her, someone to talk to and lean on as she navigated her own teenage and young adult years. But instead of letting that gap define her, she poured everything she had into her younger sisters. Being the oldest of five, she carried a weight far beyond her years, sacrificing her own youth so that we could have guidance, care, and love.

I can still see her in the kitchen, hair pulled back, sleeves rolled up, stirring pots while keeping an eye on the youngest ones doing homework at the table. The smell of her cooking filled the house, but it was not about food, it was about comfort, about making sure we felt safe, fed, and cared for.

And then there were the quiet, patient moments she gave us every single day. Braiding our hair, even when her fingers ached from chores; folding laundry while singing softly, making the house feel like home; checking our homework line by line, sometimes explaining math problems repeatedly until we got it. She did it all without complaint, as if these small acts of care were the most natural thing in the world.

When life took our parents from us, the absence was heavy. But Shelva's presence helped fill that gap. She stepped in with both firmness and gentleness—quick to correct us when we strayed, but just as quick to comfort us when we were hurting. Her voice carried weight, not because she demanded respect, but because she had already earned it.

The Book of Allison: The Wounds You Don't See

Even on her own hardest days, when she wanted to be a teenager or young adult living her own life, Shelva showed up. She cooked. She cleaned. She guided me. She listened. She carried the weight of the household and of our hearts without ever letting us feel it.

Shelva's love was not about grand gestures; it was about consistency. She was there, steady, and dependable, like a second heartbeat in the home. Her sacrifices, her guidance, and her unwavering care shaped us in ways we are still discovering today. She did not just tell us what to do, she showed us how to live with love, patience, and resilience.

I remember when she moved out of the house, I was sad and thought I would never see her again; However, she did not disappoint. Every weekend she would allow me and my younger sibling to sleep over. I was excited because the project was all that I knew and seeing her living in her own apartment outside of the projects, I thought she was rich.

To this day, I think of her as more than my sister—she was, and still is, my second mom and, she aggravates my nerve; however, how can I not still love her after all she had done for her siblings.

Shelva, if I never told you how much I appreciated everything you did for me and your younger siblings, I want to publicly say it now. I appreciate you and my love for you is itched in my heart.

Spencer L. James, Jr. — The Protector of the Family: The Third Oldest Out of Eight

Spencer was the younger brother, but he carried himself like the man of the house. When our parents separated, he didn't wait for anyone to assign him a role—he appointed himself the protector of the family. And when our father passed away, that sense of duty became even stronger. He devoted himself to our mother and made sure his sisters were always safe.

Spencer had the strength of an elephant and the presence of a lion. He walked with authority, spoke with confidence, and feared absolutely nothing. He was the kind of man who would go against an army of people all by himself if it meant protecting his family. That was just who he was—fearless, loyal, and bold in his love for family.

Though our oldest brother, Orlandrus, took on the role of caregiver, Spencer was the enforcer—the one who made sure we stayed in line and showed our mother the respect she deserved. When it came to her, Spencer didn't play. His devotion ran deep, and he carried that responsibility with pride.

And let me tell you, Spencer took his role as protector and enforcer very seriously—so seriously that he expected to be treated like the king of the house. He had his younger sisters cooking his food, ironing his clothes, combing his hair, and even doing his laundry.

He loved being waited on and pampered, and we couldn't help but spoil him. It was his way of keeping order, but also his way of showing trust in us.

We grumbled sometimes, but deep down, we loved taking care of him because he made us feel safe.

But underneath that toughness was a softer side. Spencer was a lover boy—the kind who made women stop and stare. With his smooth, dark skin, bowlegged stride, and confident smile, he didn't have to say much to capture attention.

He was a bodybuilder in his own way, strong and defined, and the women couldn't resist his charm. I still remember young women—and even some older ones—trying to bribe me and my younger sister with candy or money just to get a little information about him.

That was Spencer—protector, provider, and charmer all in one. His love was fierce, his courage unshakable, and his spirit unforgettable. Even though he's no longer here with us, I know he's watching from above.

Heaven gained one of its strongest soldiers the day Spencer left this earth and joined our parents in heaven – I'm sure he's up in heaven guarding my mother and singing with my father; they loved singing together. His spirit continues to cover and protect our family—just as he always did. I love you brother.

Sharon, Rebel Without a Cause: The Second Oldest Out of Six Sisters.

Sharon — also known as Basima, Runnie. From the moment she came into this world, I learned from my older siblings that Sharon was determined to do things her way.

She started running before she even learned how to walk — that's how she earned her nickname, Runnie. She was always in motion, always moving to her own beat. If you told her to smile, she'd give you a frown. If you told her to sit down, she'd stand right up. With Sharon, you had to say the opposite of what you really wanted if you wanted her to do it.

Growing up, she was the tomboy of all six girls — rough, tough, and cool without even trying. While most of us were inside playing with dolls, Sharon was outside climbing fences, racing the boys, proving she could hang with the best of them. And truth be told, she could do anything better than they could. That was just her way.

She didn't take nonsense from anybody. If you crossed her or someone she loved, you'd find out quickly that Sharon didn't back down. She'd fight you in a New York minute — not because she liked trouble, but because she stood for what she believed in. Either she liked you or she didn't — there was no gray area with her. And somehow, that honesty made people respect her even more.

As the years went by, life shifted, but Sharon's spirit never did. She grew into a woman who carried that same fire, only now it was mixed with love, loyalty, and deep compassion. She would give you her last dollar, cook you a meal even when her own cabinets were bare, and show up for her family no matter what.

The Book of Allison: The Wounds You Don't See

She was the type who didn't talk about what she was going to do — she just did it.

Life, though, doesn't always deal with us a fair hand. There were challenges, heartbreaks, and seasons that tested her strength. But Sharon didn't fold. She played the hand she was given — with courage, pride, and faith. What always amazed me most about her is that through every storm, every setback, and every silent battle, she never complained. Not once.

Now, at sixty years old, she lies in bed at a nursing facility. Her body may have slowed down, but not her spirit. It's still that same strong, no-nonsense, loving energy that has always defined her. When I visit, she greets me with that same familiar look that says, "I'm still here. Don't feel sorry for me." And even now, she doesn't ask for much — just love, laughter, and presence.

I often think back to how she used to protect us growing up — the way she stood up for her sisters, the way she made us laugh even in challenging times. Sharon never had a lot, but she gave what she could. She never said no when someone needed her. That kind of love is rare, and I want her to know it never went unnoticed. She deserves to know how deeply she's loved, how much she's admired, and how unforgettable her spirit truly is.

This page was written in love — for my sister Sharon, the original rebel without a cause, who taught me that strength doesn't always have to be loud, and that love doesn't always have to be perfect to be powerful.

Jackie, the Resourceful One: The Third Oldest Sister

Every family has that one person who just knows how to figure things out. The one who always has an answer, a plan, a connection, or a way through the impossible. For us, that was Jackie. Whenever we were stuck, whenever life left us staring at a closed door with no idea how to open it, we knew exactly who to call. Jackie.

Jackie had a gift for solving problems. She did not just see obstacles, she saw possibilities. While the rest of us were scratching our heads, she was already on the phone, already moving pieces, already making things happen. That was her love language: resourcefulness. She made sure we were never without a way forward.

I will never forget the time when my life hit rock bottom. I was homeless, living out of my van, with everything I owned stuffed into plastic garbage bags. Every night I parked my van in Prince and Spruce Street Projects parking lot nobody knew I was homeless and tried to convince myself that tomorrow would be better, even as hopelessness pressed down harder.

And then came the knock. I will never forget that sound—Jackie tapping on my van window, her face filled with determination, not pity.

She did not ask me how I ended up there, and she did not waste time on lectures. Instead, she smiled that matter-of-fact smile of hers and said, "Come on, I found you an apartment. Let us go. The landlord is waiting for us to sign the lease."

Just like that, my life shifted. Jackie did not just hand me hope—she drove me to it, stood beside me, and made sure I had a key in my hand before the day was done. That is who she is. She did not talk about solutions; she delivered them.

Jackie's love was not the kind that needed grand gestures. It was practical, precise, and powerful. When we needed something—paperwork filled out, a call made, a plan created—it was Jackie we turned to. And without fail, she showed up with exactly what we needed, often before we even knew how to ask.

She was the fixer, the planner, the one who made sure no problem was too big to manage. In her own way, Jackie was the glue that kept us moving forward when life tried to stall us out. However, when we did not take her advice or did as she asked - her favorite thing to say to us was "you baldheaded bitch" why you did not listen to me. I could never understand why she called all her sister's baldhead when her ponytail was the shortest of all of us.

Looking back, I realize her resourcefulness was more than just a skill—it was a kind of protection. She refused to let any of us sink, and she proved it repeatedly with her actions. That knock on the window was not just the sound of my sister showing up—it was the sound of God's grace arriving through her hands.

That is Jackie. The resourceful sister. The one who never let us stay stuck. The one we called when we needed answers. The one who always came through.

But then things changed, she needed her sibling to come through for her.

During the pandemic, Jackie was one of the ones who caught COVID. I thought I was going to lose my mind. I remember my second mom, Shelva, calling to tell me that Jackie was being rushed to the hospital—and that she wasn't allowed to go with her. My heart dropped.

I woke my husband awake, tears streaming down my face, my anxiety through the roof. I called my pastor, and he prayed for me over the phone.

I could tell my husband was exhausted, but he still sat up with me, watching me pace the floor. I walked up and down that house all night long, crying, praying, and shouting, "Oh God, Oh God!" I was pleading for a miracle.

For Thirty- five days straight, I texted Jackie, even though she couldn't respond. I prayed for her, and I prayed for me. The stress hit my body hard—I had muscle spasms from the top of my head down to my feet for three days straight.

I took three showers a day just to hide my tears so my husband and daughter wouldn't see me breaking down. Deep down, I honestly thought we were going to lose her.

But GOD!

On the thirty-fifth day, my husband came running into the house yelling, "Jackie's on the phone!" I froze. "My sister Jackie?" I asked. He nodded, smiling. I didn't even want to pick up the phone because I was afraid, I'd start crying all over again. But I had to.

When I answered, her voice was soft but hashed. She asked me questions I wasn't ready to answer. I told her, "Don't worry about anything right now. Just get well. We'll fill you in when the time is right." She had been in a coma for Thirty-five days, but God saw fit to wake her up.

Even though she survived, I still found myself mourning the version of my sister I had before the pandemic. She lost some of her memory and had to learn how to walk again. She still needs an oxygen machine to help her breathe.

Every time I saw her outside, my heart skips a beat. I was terrified of losing her again—not for a day, not for a week, not ever. But Jackie? She has always been strong-willed. She knew what was best for her.

Today, she's back to being the resourceful one living her best life, traveling, dancing her heart out, volunteering, and being a blessing to everyone she meets. Watching her thrive reminds me of one thing I'll never forget: when man says it's over, God still has the final say.

You can find her book on Amazon "While I Was Under Surviving COVID-19" Thirty-Five Days of Peace." She shares the dreams she had will in a comma and the experience she had during rehabilitation.

My Sister Dorothea – The One Who Danced to Her Own Beat: The Middle Sister.

Dorothea, also known as Latifah, or simply "La."

Since we were kids, Dorothea always did things off the beaten path. Whatever people expected her not to do, that's exactly what she would do—and she'd do it boldly, without hesitation. She had a way of pulling you into her adventures too, especially my younger sister Zanna and me. Half the time, I couldn't tell if we followed her because we were scared to say no or because deep down, we wanted to join in on the fun.

Either way, when La made up her mind to do something, nothing or no one could stop her. Being the August Virgo that she is, she stands firm in her decisions, proud, confident, and unapologetic. If given the chance to do it all again, I'm sure she'd make the same choices twice, without a blink.

I could never quite tell if Dorothea did things for attention or simply because she wanted to. Growing up, she was one of the darker-skinned siblings, and I often wondered if she ever felt like the "black sheep" among the girls. But the truth couldn't be further from that. I grew up right under her, watching her closely, and to me—she was the prettiest of us all.

Her rich, dark skin, bright white teeth, and radiant smile were unmatched. She stood out naturally, even when she didn't try. Maybe she didn't realize she never had to fight for attention—there were eight of us, and we were all just trying to be seen in our own way—but her light always found its way through.

Fast forward to adulthood—life has a way of dealing with each of us our own hand. We all face challenges and carry burdens, wounds that no one else can see. Yet, through it all, Dorothea has continued to rise.

She's a fierce protector of her children and a devoted grandmother who doesn't hesitate to check anyone who crosses that line. That's just La—bold, loyal, and full of heart.

She's known pain too. The tragic loss of her eldest son, Terrance, affectionately known as Tee-Tee, was a wound that cut deep. His life was taken senselessly while he was simply doing his job—a pain no mother should ever have to bear. Rest in peace, Tee-Tee. You are forever loved, and your spirit lives on through all of us.

Even after such heartbreak, La kept marching—right to the rhythm of her own drum, just as she always has. I admire her strength, her fire, and her unwavering love for her family.

I love you, my dark-skinned queen. Keep marching, keep shining, and never forget how much you are loved.

My Sister Zanna – My Built-In Best Friend: The Baby of the Bunch.

Growing up, Zanna and I were more than sisters — we were best friends. Inseparable. We did everything together, so much so that everyone thought we were twins. We dressed alike, walked alike, talked alike, and finished each other's sentences.

Wherever you saw one of us, you could bet the other wasn't far behind. Even as we got older, our bond stayed strong. She was a sophomore in school when I was a senior, but that never stopped us from acting like we were still joined at the hip.

If one of us got in trouble, we both got in trouble. There was no such thing as just one of us being punished — we were a package deal. And when one of us was sick, it was like we both felt it. I couldn't physically feel her pain, but I carried it with me. We worried about each other constantly.

There was something about our connection that was deep, unspoken, and unbreakable. We shared a room, a bed, and shared secrets that will forever stay between us — secrets only sisters, only best friends, could understand.

Zanna was spoiled in the sweetest way. Everybody loved her — those deep dimples and her big, expressive "Popeyes" made her unforgettable. She had a personality that drew people in, and no matter where we went, she was the one who got all the attention.

I'd be lying if I said I didn't feel overlooked sometimes when she was around. My oldest sister Shelva's friends adored Zanna too — they'd give her gifts, took her to events, and shower her with love. But even when I felt invisible in her shadow, I couldn't help but love her more. That was my sister, my other half, my heart.

As time passed, life did what it always does — it grew us up and led us in different directions. We found our independence, started our careers, built our families, and began carving out our own identities. We weren't "the twins" anymore, but the bond never left. Even now, Zanna still has that baby-of-the-bunch energy, expecting her older siblings to jump when she calls. And I have to remind her — lovingly, of course — that we're not kids anymore. We're grown women now, both married, both mothers, both holding our own.

Still, when she needs me, I'm there — no questions asked. Because that's what sisters do. No matter how old we get, no matter how far life takes us, I'll always be right there to fill in that gap with the same love I've had for her since we were little girls sharing a room, a bed, and a lifetime of laughter.

I love you, Zanna — my sister, my twin in spirit, my forever best friend.

And Then There Was Me, Allison – The Quiet One Who Became "The One"

And then there was Allison — the second youngest of seven sisters. The quiet one. The one who didn't talk much, who preferred peace over noise and observation over attention. The one who didn't like to get her hands dirty, who could sit for hours just staring out the window, daydreaming about life beyond the block, beyond the noise, beyond the moment. My sisters would call me special in a negative sense, and to this day some of them still do in a humorous way.

While my sisters laughed loud, argued hard, and took up space, I often found comfort in the background. Silence was my language, and imagination was my friend. People mistook my quietness for weakness, but silence has a strength of its own — a strength that listens, learns, and waits for its time. People that I grew up with often connect with me on social media and remind me how quiet I used to be.

I still remember my father looking at me one day and saying, "You're the one." At the time, I didn't fully understand what he meant. I just knew that being the one sounded important, even special. But life would soon show me that being the one came with a heavy weight. It meant carrying things that others couldn't see. It meant enduring trials that would break most people. It meant walking through pain that would one day become my purpose.

I didn't know that the one would be the one who'd have to grow up faster, love harder, and learn to stand alone. I didn't know the one would be tested in ways that would shape her into a woman of strength, faith, and resilience. But here I am — still standing.

The Book of Allison: The Wounds You Don't See

The quiet girl who once stared out the window became the woman who learned to see beyond her circumstances. The one who didn't like getting her hands dirty became the woman willing to roll up her sleeves and advocate for others. The one who rarely spoke found her voice — not to talk, but to lead, to heal, to serve, and to inspire.

I didn't choose to be the one — but I've learned to embrace it. Every hardship, every setback, every moment of doubt has prepared me for my purpose. I am the one who beat the odds. The one who turned pain into power. The one who turned struggle into service.

And as my story continues, I carry every lesson, every scar, and every bit of love from my siblings who shaped me — because before I was "the one," I was one of them.

Chapter One Workbook: The Foundation We Stand On

Scripture: Psalm 133:1 NIV

Summary:

This chapter explores the deep struggles and hidden wounds tied to this theme. It invites you to reflect honestly and discover healing through faith, resilience, and the power of second chances.

Reflection Questions:

1. What role has your family played in your healing journey?
2. Who do you consider your chosen family?

Activity: Family Tree of Support

Draw or list the people (bloodline or chosen) who give you strength.

Affirmation:

"I am not my past. I am my strength."

Journal Space:

_____
_____
_____
_____
_____
_____

The Book of Allison: The Wounds You Don't See

Chapter 2

Written by Allison K. James – Frison

(Certain trivial subdivisions written in this chapter were by Nicole K. Horn Shelton.)

Every Apology Came with a Scar

Domestic Violence

Introduction:

Domestic violence is often hidden behind closed doors, silent in its terrors, and invisible to those who have not experienced it firsthand. Yet its impact reaches far beyond the immediate victim—it ripples through families, communities, and generations. For me, understanding domestic violence was not witnessing it in society, it was personal. It was about recognizing the patterns, the fear, and the quiet resilience required to survive each day.

It is a story of pain, but also of courage: the courage to acknowledge the truth, seek help, and reclaim one's life. This chapter is not merely an account of abuse—it is a testament to survival. It explores the emotional, psychological, and at times, physical toll of domestic violence, and the strength it takes to break free from the cycles that try to define us.

I can still hear my mom's words echoing in my ear, even louder now that she is no longer here: "As long as I'm alive, you'll always have a place to stay." She drilled it into me over and over: Never date a man who hits you. Because I was not anyone's personal punching bag, or a target for their training.

The Book of Allison: The Wounds You Don't See

But did I listen? No. Like any other town, my neighborhood had its rough areas, places where the air seemed to hum with tension, and the sound of fights and sirens blended into the background.

I avoided them as best I could. But one day, my mom asked me to go to the neighborhood pharmacy to buy a money order. As I walked, I saw two female friends from another building. They called out to me. Normally, I would've kept walking, avoiding the chaos, but something made me turn around and go over.

We were talking when I saw him—a tall, light-skinned, good-looking guy who appeared like a flash out of nowhere. Time seemed to slow. My heart pounded, and I could not seem to look away. He wore an orange tank top, matching shorts, and had a low haircut that made him stand out even more. He walked through the crowd, and I was frozen, just staring at him.

I asked one of my friends, "Who is that?" She raised an eyebrow, like I was crazy. "That's Eddie, one of the Blue's brothers. How do you not know him?" I did not know, but at that moment, I just knew—he was going to be my husband. After that day, I started spending more time in the very area I had spent years avoiding. I dressed up, hoping he would notice me, though for a while, I did not see him again. Then, one day, as I came home from work, I saw a fight break out behind one of the buildings.

Normally, I would have kept walking in the opposite direction, but today, I was searching for Eddie. And there he was. My future husband, standing in chaos like he was meant to be there. The world stopped again. And I could not look away.

Fast forward two weeks. My mom sends me to the pharmacy again, this time to play her pick-its. And there he was: Eddie. He was yelling at a little girl, and as I listened, I realized she was his daughter, crying for ice cream. After a moment, Eddie stepped away to play his pick-its.

I quickly wrote my phone number on a piece of paper and walked over to his daughter.

I asked her "If you give your dad my number I will buy you some ice cream." She agreed, and I left the store, my heart racing. As I walked home, I could not help but smile. But then it hit me—I had just entrusted my fate to a young child, and neither time I had seen Eddie, I had he spoken a word to me. And to make matters worse, I had forgotten to play my mom's pick-its. When I got home without them, she cussed me out. I did not care though because I was too excited about the chance to talk to Eddie.

A few weeks passed, but finally, his daughter came through. I was walking into the house when the phone rang—it was Eddie. We talked for about 15 minutes, and I could not stop smiling. I knew he could hear it in my voice. Before hanging up, he asked if I would like to go bowling on Friday. I agreed, but the wait felt like it was forever. Those four days were the longest of my life, and my smile never faded.

Finally, Friday arrived. He pulled up in a black Cadillac Escalade, blasting music. I was so excited I walked toward his truck slowly, looking around to see who was watching. I felt like everyone was looking at me, and in my head, I was walking like a top model, confident and sexy.

From that night on, we were inseparable for the next seven years, sometimes on and sometimes off. He showered me with gifts, everything I wanted and more. But what I did not know was that the love I had dreamed of came with a price. Eddie was an alcoholic. I had vowed never to drink or date someone who drank, but soon, I was spending my nights in bars with him. I started drinking with him, and eventually, I became an alcoholic too.

The Book of Allison: The Wounds You Don't See

My drinking spiraled out of control. I would black out, get kicked out of bars, and still manage to drag myself to work every day. I kept a mini bar by my bed and made sure to have a drink before doing anything else. But then the violence started, and from there, everything began to change.

One day, while driving down Hillside Ave in Hillside, we stopped at a light. Without warning, Eddie grabbed my face and bit me underneath my eye. The pain was instant. He then reached into the glove compartment, pulled out a screwdriver, and pointed it at me. Blood ran down my face, soaking into my blouse, but I did not say a word.

I was terrified. When the light turned green, I drove on like nothing had happened, even as blood dripped from my cheek. I dropped him off at our destination and went home alone. There, I cleaned myself up, placing a band-aid over the scar that would join so many others. I kept it hidden in the place I had learned to protect, and never talk about, the wounds you don't see.

For years, I wore sunglasses—indoors, outdoors, day and night—like they were my armor. I never left home without them. But no matter how much I hid behind them, the scar never went away. Every time I looked in the mirror, the scar was a constant reminder of who I was, who I had become. A reminder that no one else could see the wounds I carried, but I could not escape.

In the summer we traveled to Atlanta, during a couple's getaway that was anything but romantic, I proposed to him. We were both drunk, but it was not just the alcohol that pushed me to do it, it was love, or at least the desperate hope that he would choose me.

I did not even get a clear answer. He did not say yes, but he accepted the ring, and for me, that was enough. He wore his ring, until he lost his at work. After that, neither of us bothered to replace it, and I stopped asking him about it.

Two Shifts Day & Night

Not long after my proposal, I discovered Eddie was seeing someone else. He had been with her all along—two lives, two relationships, running parallel. During the day, he would be with her, and at night, he would spend time with me. She worked evenings, so I was on the "night shift." It was a game to him, and I was just another piece on his board. When I found out, everything changed.

The daytime girlfriend didn't just hide in the shadow she flaunted it. She stole his car keys while he slept, then drove to the neighborhood, blasting music for everyone to hear, for everyone to see her in his truck. She didn't know what I looked like, but I knew exactly what she was doing. It was a declaration: I'm the one who's winning now.

I was outside when I saw her, and I was angry—furious. I was on a mission to get answers, to demand my place, but when I tried reaching Eddie, he ignored me. I blew up his beeper, added "911" after my number—an emergency. But of course, he didn't answer. That only made my rage burn hotter.

I remember pacing the block, my hands shaking, trying to hold it together but ready to lose it all at the same time. I wanted to pull up, make a scene, let her and everybody else know who I was. I wasn't about to be played or embarrassed. I was the one who held him down, the one who cooked, cleaned, and loved him when nobody else would. And this is how he repaid me?

I walked to that truck, my heart beating out my chest. She was still sitting there like she owned it, like she owned him. For a second, I thought about snatching that door open, but I stopped.

The Book of Allison: The Wounds You Don't See

Not because I wasn't about it, but because I realized in that second, she wasn't the one who betrayed me—he was. And that hurt worse than anything, the silent wound.

I turned around, walked off, but every step felt like fire. That was the night something in me shifted. I wasn't the same after that. You don't come back the same after watching love turn into humiliation right in front of your face. That night I barely slept. I laid there staring at the ceiling, my mind running circles around every lie he told me, every time he looked at me in my face and said I was the only one. My chest was tight, my pride was bruised, but more than anything, I felt like played. You don't come back from that kind of disrespect easily.

By morning, I was done crying. I wanted answers. I pulled up to his spot unannounced—no call, no warning. He opened the door acting like nothing happened, like I didn't just see another woman riding around in his truck. The nerve of him. He tried to smile, tried to flip it on me, talking about, "You always tripping,' Alli." That's when I lost it. All the pain, the anger, the humiliation came up at once.

I told him straight up, "Don't play with me. I know everything." He tried to deny it, then got quiet, looking down like a man caught in a lie with no words left to hide behind. I could feel the tension in the room shift. For a minute, I didn't know if I wanted to slap him, cry, or just walk away. But I did none of that. I just stood there, staring at him, realizing this wasn't love, it was control. He wanted both of us, wanted to be worshiped, wanted to have his cake and eat it too.

I walked out that day with nothing but my pride and my pain, but I walked out. I didn't look back. My hands were shaking, but my spirit was steady. That was the last time I let a man make me feel like I had to fight for a spot that already belonged to me.

After that, my love got colder, my heart got smarter, and my peace became something I protected like my life depended on it. Walking away was only the first step. Healing was the hard part. People think once you leave, you're free—but they don't see the nights you replay everything in your head, asking yourself how you didn't see the signs, how you let somebody break you down like that. I had to face that mirror and admit I wasn't just angry, I was hurt. Deep hurt. The kind that sits in your chest like a brick.

For a while, I moved like nothing bothered me. I went to work, smiled, laughed with friends, acted like life was good—but inside, I was still bleeding. Every time my phone rang, I half-expected it to be him. I hated that part of me still wanted him to call, still wanted an apology that I knew would never come. That's when I realized healing wasn't about forgetting—it was about letting go of the fantasy I created in my head.

Some days I cried so hard my body felt weak. Other days I felt unstoppable, like I finally had control again. It came in waves—anger, sadness, peace, then right back to anger. But I kept showing up for myself. I started, sitting in silence instead of chaos. Slowly, I started to recognize the woman in the mirror again—not the one who begged to be chosen, but the one who finally chose herself.

It wasn't pretty. Healing never is. It's lonely, it's confusing, and sometimes it hurts more than the relationship ever did. But every day I got a little stronger. I learned to find peace in my own space, to move without needing validation. My love for myself became louder than the pain he left behind.

And when I finally looked back, I didn't see a broken woman anymore—I saw a survivor, still standing, still shining, still here. That was the rebirth. The moment I stopped chasing closure and started creating peace.

The moment I stopped needing to be loved and started learning to love myself. Every scar, every tear, every sleepless night became part of my testimony. I just didn't survive what broke me, I rose from it, so I thought. I later found out that Eddie was incarcerated, the reason why, I was not receiving any calls from him.

Mustafa

Two years had passed with Eddie still in jail when I met Mustafa— "Mu" as everyone called him. We worked together, and he made it a point to come into my office every day to use the copy machine. He charmed the hell out of me with his gifts, smooth demeanor, mature conversations. Before I knew it, things had escalated quickly.

We were living together for two years; swept up in a whirlwind I could not understand at the time. Somehow, Mu managed to gain control over me, and I was blind to it. Whatever he said, I did. Whatever he asked for, I delivered—perfectly, or else there was hell to pay, a beaten was in the atmosphere sometimes I tried to prepare myself for the abuse; however, he never seemed to matter, the physical, emotional, and financial abuse escalated as time went on.

I worked hard every day, but on payday, I never saw the fruits of my labor. Mu made sure I handed over my paycheck, and I had no say in it.

I was not allowed to have guests at our home, and when I was allowed to go out, I had a strict curfew. I always ended up with the same taxi driver, and I later learned the driver was reporting my whereabouts back to him.

One time, I was ironing my clothes to go out with friends. Mu told me I could not go, and I told him I was going anyway. He grabbed the very iron I was using and burned my hand.

That was not enough for him. He punched me in the gut, and I hit the floor. Since then, I have never used a iron again. People, places and things are triggers.

Mu did not eat pork, and one of my guilty pleasures was Twinkies. One day, he saw them on the counter, and without a word, took them out of the box, unwrapped them, and smacked me in the face with them. I went into the bathroom to clean my face and ate every Twinkie that was smeared on my face, I thought I had won that battle, because those Twinkies gave me so much joy, I was doing something that he hated eating pork. I learned to walk on eggshells, fearing his next move.

I was not even allowed to warm his food in the microwave. The oven had to be preheated to the exact temperature ten minutes before he came home, so his food was perfect when he arrived. If I did not get it exactly right, the punishment would be severe. Something in the house would be broken because of him throwing an object at me.

I believed my neighbor knew about the abuse; because every time I left out for work, she was walking out her door at the exact same time asking me if I was ok, I would always say yes looking down at the floor ashamed. In my mind I wanted to ask her to call the police next time she heard me crying or screaming; however, I did not want to put her in danger.

Mu attended my mother's funeral with me. During the repast, I fixed a plate for one of the attendees. He accused me of cheating because of it. When we got home, the accusations continued. He did not believe my explanations, and that turned into violence.

The Book of Allison: The Wounds You Don't See

I had just buried my mother, and here he was, accusing me of nonsense. My emotions were overwhelming. I fought back—I grabbed whatever was within arm's reach. The lamp, the iron (the same one he burned me with), I cleared the dresser by throwing everything at him. But no matter how hard I fought, he always won.

The anger I felt was not just because he accused me of an affair. It was because I had not seen my mother in over a month. He had given me a black eye, and I could not bear the thought of her seeing me like that. My mother used to bring young ladies into our house and apply makeup to their scars she would remind them that love does not hurt and sitting outside displacing bruises on our body was not appropriate.

I didn't want to be one of those young ladies that sat at my mother's kitchen table applying makeup on them to cover up the bruises. However, hiding from my mother while being abused keeps me from seeing her alive. The next time I saw her, it was in a casket at her going home service.

So, when I fought back, it was not just about defending myself. It was about all the times I did not say "yes" when my mother asked me if Mu was hitting on me. Maybe, had I been honest with her, she could have saved me from the brutality that followed.

Every day, I asked myself, how can I escape this man?

The phone call gave me a way out.

Normally, a 3 a.m. phone call was dreadful and likely to bring tears. But not this one. This phone call was my way out. It was one of Mu's friends, calling to tell me that Mu had been arrested and was in jail.

As soon as we hung up, I packed what I could, grabbed my things as quickly as possible, and left. I did not look back. However, the fear of him getting released on bail and finding out where I was at haunted me more than the abuse.

Years later, eighteen years later to be exact, I was on Broad Street in Newark getting my hair done. When I finished, I walked across the street to get something to eat, I did not pay attention to the customers in the store. I heard someone say, "Is that Allison, Allison James?" I did not recognize this person. He looked thinner, some of his teeth were missing, his hair was uncut, and hygiene was poor. He called my name, and I stared, wondering how he knew it. He said, "It's me — Mu." I snapped back, "Oh — the one who used to beat the dog shit out of me, burned me with an iron, used me as a punching bag and took my paycheck every week" He looked at me and said, "Allison, I never hit you or did any of those things to you."

I wanted to beat his ass with my purse and make him remember. He asked me for a ride home and for the first time I said no to him. It felt good to say it. In the past, saying no would have resulted in me getting beaten, but on this day, I took back the power he had held for eighteen years of me praying I would never run into him. I walked away feeling powerful, head held high, leaving him there to find his next victim.

My family members and friends use to call me all the time and say, "I ran into Mu he asked about you." My response was always the same "please do not give him my phone number or address." I was still hiding from him all those years; however, my day came, and I was able to exhale and to me, my no-meaning justice was served. I got in my car and texted my therapist for a session, I could not wait to tell her what had just happened.

The Book of Allison: The Wounds You Don't See

Eddie is released.

After three long years, he was released from prison, and we were right back together as if nothing ever happened. Y'all already know Eddie was my soulmate in my head. Yes, we fought and made up, but it felt different this time. I would tell myself repeatedly this time it will be different it would be better, this time, this time, this time; however, it was not. But he was my soulmate, and I loved him.

Everyone from the neighborhood knew Ali and Eddie were together. They never liked me being with Mu. I guess if they had to choose the lesser evil of the two, it would be Eddie.

But there came a day when I decided I had had enough. I was tired. Tired of the abuse, the hitting, the yelling, the biting—all of it. Eddie became aggressive towards me while we were outside, he was intoxicated. We began to argue, and before I knew it, he kicked me with his steel-toe boots. The pain was unbearable. I drove myself home.

I started cooking dinner, trying to focus on anything other than the sting of the blows. But when he arrived, the argument continued. He was drunk, and the alcohol only made his behavior worse. He called me names, yelled at me, berated me. The plate of food was already in my hand, ready to serve him, but at that moment, all I wanted was for him to stop. The thought of throwing the plate crossed my mind—not to hurt him, but to startle him, to shut him up, if just for a moment.

The yelling grew louder and louder, and in that instant, I made the decision. I turned to throw the plate at him, hoping the crash would quiet him. But in a flash, he moved toward me, and everything changed. It all happened in slow motion, like a nightmare I could not wake up from.

I can still hear the pounding of my heart, drowning out everything else. The plate shattered, our scream echoed and then came the blood.

For a moment, we both seemed stunned, even in shock. But as the realization set in, the fight began. We did not stop until he saw our own blood. Yes, I was tired—tired of the abuse, tired of the emotional and physical toll. But hurting him was not my intention. All I wanted was silence, for him to stop yelling, to stop the insults.

As I ran out of the house, a part of me realized I was not just running from him. I was running from what I could become in this situation—an angry and bitter woman with no hope left. The fear of the unknown weighed heavily on me. We both were hurt, there was blood, and I did not know where it was coming from. The questions that were running through my mind. "What if he told the police, it was me? Would he press charges just to save himself? Would I have to bear the weight of my mistake alone?"

I ran to a hotel and stayed there for a few days, unsure of what to do next. When I returned to our apartment, I expected him to kick me out. But he did not. To my surprise, Eddie never asked me to leave. I was relieved. The thought of being separated from him terrified me. It triggered those childhood memories of my parents' separation, which feeling of abandonment that haunted me.

I stayed with him. Even when everything in me screamed to leave, I stayed. I convinced myself that the pain of being alone was worse than the abuse. I kept telling myself it was not healthy, but I loved him. I stayed, because at that moment, I was afraid of what might happen if I did not stay. The pain of being alone felt unbearable, and the love I had for him—no matter how twisted it was—kept me there.

This emotional rollercoaster we were on was insane. One minute, I was happy, laughing, feeling like everything was okay. The next, I was hurting, wondering if the laughter would trigger his rage. I did not know if laughing too loud, or too long would set him off. I did not know if washing the dishes or cooking his meal "wrong" would lead to a slap or a punch. Every action felt like a calculated risk, but I stayed.

I loved him. I loved him because despite everything, he wanted me to stay, and I wanted to stay. He gave me stability, security, something I had craved for so long. The fear of losing that outweighed everything else. Even when I knew deep down that the relationship was not healthy, I stayed because in my mind, I could not see a way out.

However, there was a pleasant side of him that I loved even more. I watched him carry grocery for elder women that lived in the area, have community BBQs for families and loaded up charter buses to take youth to Six Flags this allowed them to have a great summer if only for a day. I watched him pay rent for families who received eviction notices. Please note that this is not an excuse for how we treated each other; however, these are some of the reasons why I loved him.

While drafting this book he came to me in a dream. However, his name was not Eddie. When I woke up, I could not remember the name everyone was calling him. However, what I took away from the dream was him giving me the OK to finish this book and tell my story.

Eddie and I had another fight—there were so many, I could not even remember what it was about anymore. But this time, he called the police. When the officer arrived, he told us that one of us had to leave.

My name was not on the lease, I did not have any bills tied to the address, so it was clear whoever had to go it was me. I packed what I could, stuffing my things into black garbage bags inot my van, and went to stay with my friend Melissa. But that situation did not last long. The next day, while I was at work, yes, I had a temporary job; however, it was a job. Melissa stole and sold most of my belongings. I had nowhere else to go, so I ended up sleeping in my van.

This was the beginning of my homelessness. It was not ideal, but it felt safer than the uncertainty of living in someone else's home, and in the neighborhood that I grew up in, no one would question it. People slept in their cars all the time. No one knew I was homeless, not even me, sometimes; because nothing changed besides my living arrangements, I went on with my daily routine. Melissa may have stolen my things, but she allowed me to shower and get dressed at her place every day before work. It was the bare minimum, but at that time, it was all I had.

One day, while I was in my van sleeping, I heard a knock on the window. It was my sister Jackie, you all remember her, the resourceful sister. She said, "Come on, I found an apartment for you." I looked at her, confused, and disoriented, and she repeated, "Don't you need a place to live?" Without thinking, I nodded through tear-filled eyes and said, "Yes." At that moment I realized that I was ashamed of who I was and embarrassed that my life was falling apart and I needed my parents' existence in this moment more than anything in this world.

The thought of finally having my own place filled me with some relief, and for a moment, I allowed myself to dream. The apartment was above a storefront, but I did not care. It was mine. I had a space to call my own, something I had not had in so long.

I asked a guy I knew to help me assemble my bed, hang the shower rod, set up the blinds. He agreed, but I had made a quick run to the store for a screwdriver. When I returned, everything was set up, but he was gone. I did not think much of it—until the next morning.

As I woke up, started cooking breakfast in my own space I saw a piece of paper slid under my door. It was an eviction notice. I had thirty days to move out.

I stood there, frozen, trying to understand what had just happened. It did not seem real. I called the landlord, who explained that the man I had let into my apartment the previous night had robbed the neighbor next door. He was caught on camera, stealing her jewelry and money. The landlord told me it was not my fault, but because of the company I kept, I was no longer allowed to stay.

My heart sank. My stomach twisted in knots. I was angry—angry at him, but mostly angry at myself for once again finding myself in an uncompromising situation and trusting everyone with my livelihood. I had just one night of peace, of thinking I might finally have a place to call my own, and now I was being told to leave. The only option left was my van again.

I could not understand why I kept putting myself in these situations. All I wanted was stability, security, a life that did not feel like I was constantly running away from one disaster to the next. But no matter how much I wanted to break free, the universe always threw another hurdle in my way.

Salt Came with No Pepper.

I moved so many times and lived with just as many people that I do not even recall the border. But at this point in my life, I was single and living in my own apartment.

Unfortunately, I was still hanging in bars — the one on Messy Ave. This is where I met Salt. From the beginning I suspected he was up to no good, but I ignored the signs. Early on, Salt always tried to move in with me. He was the epitome of "wherever he laid his hat was his home."

He stayed with his children's mother off and on, but for the life of me I could not understand why he did not live with his parents; they had a nice big house in Elizabeth. In my opinion, he was homeless. I recognized the signs, and I understood how it felt to live without an address.

Against my better judgment, after two years of dating, I allowed Salt to move in with me. We fought constantly, but Salt bore the brunt of the anger I carried from previous abuse. I carried my shield and vowed never to be anyone's victim again.

One day I got a phone call from a friend who was depressed after losing a loved one to gun violence. Because I had experienced that kind of loss, I went to her house to show support.

We decided to go to the bar and drink the pain away. After drinking, crying, and trading stories, she dropped me off at home and the domestic violence started as soon as I walked into the door.

The Book of Allison: The Wounds You Don't See

Sleep Was the Only Thing on My Mind

All I wanted to do was sleep, but for some reason Salt chose that moment to pick a fight. I was intoxicated and his strength far outweighed mine. He pushed me, shoved me, then pinned me down on the bed, covered my face with a pillow, and began to smother me, as he laughed as if it was a joke. I fought to push him off and screamed that I could not breathe.

When he finally removed the pillow, I gasped for air and totally freaked out. I could not stop screaming, but I knew I had to get out of the house before things got worse. I called family members to get me, but at 1:00 a.m. no one answered.

All I could think was I need to get to safety, not form him but for myself. I ran out of the house on one of the coldest winter nights without a coat. I was wearing one slipper, and a Timberland boot on the other foot, but I was determined to get somewhere safe.

I speed-walked with no destination in mind. By the time I reached Springfield Ave, someone called my name. I threw up my fist, ready to defend myself — but thank God it was my oldest sister, my second mom Shelva and her husband. They put me in the back seat of their car and took me to my youngest sister Zanna's house.

I could not stop yelling, screaming, and rocking back and forth. I could hear them talk among themselves, trying to piece together what had happened. They called my friend Renée, who had dropped me off earlier, and put the call on speaker. Renée told them I had been fine when she dropped me off at home.

Shelva and her husband questioned Renée like she was on trial, but Renée's story did not change. After the call, Shelva's husband suggested they call an ambulance, but Shelva said no — she stated, "She's not trying to harm herself or anyone else.

If we call the EMS, we may never get our sister back the way she was" They would watch me through the night and let me sleep it off. When I woke up all my sisters were there protecting me and watching me.

I do not know what time I finally stopped yelling and rocking, but eventually I fell asleep. When I woke up, I asked the time and Jackie said it was 7 a.m., I begged her to take me home so I could get ready for work like nothing happened the day before.

I woke feeling oddly peaceful, as if a weight had been lifted from my shoulders. I went home, took a shower, dressed in my designer clothes, put my mink on, and went to work as if the previous night had never taken place. Looking back, I know now that night was a mental breakdown — one I had hidden from the world and from myself far too long.

A few days later, I realized I had finally mourned the loss of my parents and the death of my father, and Mu. I had carried that grief for fifteen years without mourning because trauma kept piling on. I had always put grieving on the back burner to deal with whatever new trauma showed up.

Salt and I were still together; however, not living together. Salt's best friend got married, and because we fought often, his friend did not want to invite us. We promised we would be on our best behavior. That lasted halfway through the event.

During the reception, Salt went outside to smoke and left his phone on the table. It rang, and I answered it. I found out he was expecting a baby.

When he came back inside, I confronted him and of course he denied it. I threw a glass of water at him and punched him in the face.

I left the reception and went outside to call a taxi. Before it arrived, Salt came out talking shit and I beat the hell out of him. The news traveled fast — before I could get home, my sister Jackie called and said she had heard I beat Salt up at a wedding.

"Not at a wedding, Allison," Jackie said, and we started laughing. That was the day I knew for sure I was never going to be a victim of domestic violence again, and it was.

My Perspective

Domestic violence left more than physical scars. It carved deep questions into my soul:

Was I worth loving without pain?

Could I trust a hand that did not hurt me?

Is it possible to believe in a gentle touch, instead of bracing myself for the hand that's ready to harm?

The hardest part was leaving—it was believing I deserved to. But I did. I deserved to accept kindness without suspicion. I deserved to feel comfort without flinching. I deserved to trust that not every hand reaching for me carries harm.

With each day I refused to return, I began to reclaim my name, my voice, and my future.

I can finally exhale the air from my lungs that I have been too afraid to release.

Each new struggle became easier to hide. I could not hide the bruise under my eye, no matter how much makeup I used, or the Band-Aid over a fresh wound.

But the truth was—each scar, each bruise, left an indelible mark on my heart, a mark that whispered a story of perseverance. Despite what life had taken from me; it could not steal my will to survive.

Today, I am one course away from becoming a certified Domestic Violence Advocate. Working with parents/women who need to know that they can survive, they can live without pain, that love does not hurt, it heals, it's soft, it's visible in the way your partner touches you, talks to you and not just in public however, in private where it matters the most.

There are seven types of domestic violence abuse which one if any do you identify with? Don't just read the definitions, seek help and closure.

- Physical abuse
- Sexual abuse
- Emotional abuse
- Economic abuse
- Psychological abuse
- Technological abuse
- Paternal Alienation

The Book of Allison: The Wounds You Don't See

Chapter 2 Workbook: Every Apology Came with a Scar: Domestic Violence

Scripture: Psalm 121:1–2 NIV

Summary:

This chapter explores the deep struggles and hidden wounds tied to this theme. It invites you to reflect honestly and discover healing through faith, resilience, and the power of second chances.

Reflection Questions:

1. How have apologies impacted your healing journey?
2. What scars (emotional or physical) do you carry, and how do you cope with them?

Activity: My Healing Shield

Draw or write five things that protect you when triggers appear.

Affirmation:

"I am not my past. I am my strength."

Journal Space:

_____
_____
_____
_____
_____

Chapter 3

Written by Allison K. James – Frison

(Certain trivial subdivisions written in this chapter were by Nicole K. Horn Shelton.)

Everything I Own – In a Garbage Bag

Homelessness

Introduction:

Hearing the word homelessness is easy, it is something you think happens to someone else. But no, it was once my reality. Homelessness is more than not having a roof over your head. It is the absence of a place of your own, the absence of peace of mind, and the absence of security. It is not just what we see on TV or read about; it is the truth of so many lives.

Behind every homeless person, there is a story of dreams, hopes, and a place once called home. Life, however, took a turn, and those dreams faded. But even through struggle, there is always a story of resilience. It became part of my journey to my divinely appointed destination.

Five years after my mom passed away, I experienced homelessness for the first time. I no longer had her home to return to. Her presence was my safety net. I never imagined a time when I would be without it. On the outside, I looked like I had it together—designer clothes, mink coats, five-hundred-dollar jeans and designer bags. But inside, I was hurting, grieving, crying. I dared not let anyone see my pain.

I slept on sofas, shared beds with family members' children, friends' sofas, my van and was repeatedly evicted. I was at my lowest, but I was good at pretending.

At some point, the chaos in my mind stopped racing, and the full weight of my situation crept in. I was homeless. Though it did not look like the images we see on the streets, I fell into the category of "Hidden Homelessness."

According to my research, hidden homelessness, also known as invisible homelessness, refers to individuals who are not visibly homeless or counted in official statistics.

This includes people who couch surf, temporarily staying with friends or family, or living in overcrowded or unsuitable conditions. They may be at risk of homelessness but are not yet experiencing the more obvious forms of it.

I had so many emotions, fear, uncertainty, shame, isolation, hopelessness. Fear and uncertainty dominated my thoughts. I did not know when the last day would come, the last day someone would take me in. Eviction after eviction, for reasons beyond my control, became my pattern.

Shame filled my heart. I could not let anyone know the truth behind my life. Isolation became my shield. I locked myself away, avoiding conflict, not wanting to risk being kicked out again. I began to question if I would ever find a way to become self-sufficient or secure a place to call my own.

The exhaustion from constantly moving, packing, and unpacking, renting U-Haul trucks, and just trying to keep things together weighed me down. Trust became a distant memory. Who could I trust with my secret? Could I leave my belongings anywhere without fearing they would be taken?

I hid my homelessness from the world. I showed up to work with a smile, greeting everyone as if I had slept in a king-sized bed the night before, as if everything were fine. I learned to mask my pain, to function as though nothing was wrong. My mantra became: "Hush up Allison don't piss anyone off you need this bed."

Hiding my truth became second nature. I had hidden my feelings about my parents' separation, buried the trauma of child abuse, concealed the marks of domestic violence. I even concealed the betrayals from friends who stole from me and placed me in compromising situations.

Homelessness doesn't always look like sleeping on a sidewalk or pushing a cart down a city street. Sometimes, it looks like a woman who wakes up at 3:00 a.m., quietly gets dressed in the dark so she doesn't disturb the strangers she is forced to share a room with, and slips out into the night praying she makes it to work safely. That was me.

Between Counties, Between Hope

When I used up all my resources in Essex County, I found myself in Burlington County, I had nowhere else to go, I wanted to be as far away from Essex as I could be looking for hope. The doors I knocked on in the past were no longer opening for me. I was exhausted — spiritually, mentally, emotionally — and I found myself leaning on sheer survival, not choice. That move wasn't a fresh start. It was another battle.

I rented another room out of someone's house I didn't even know because it was all I could manage, but "room" is too generous of a word. I shared a space with five other people I had never met before, each fighting their own demons and instability.

Privacy didn't exist. Silence didn't exist. Safety didn't exist. I slept lightly, always alert, always listening, always aware that anything could happen and ready to fight for my life.

My mornings began in darkness. I'd rise at 3:00 a.m., wash up quickly, and be out the door before the world opened its eyes. I traveled from Burlington County to Essex County to Bergen County like a ghost in motion — bus to train, train to bus — hours across cities to show up at work with a smile on my face, pretending everything was fine. I was doing what I had to do to keep my job, because losing that would have meant losing the last piece of structure I had left.

The streets weren't safe for a woman at that hour. I walked fast and prayed even faster. There were nights I'd rehearse what I would say or do if I was approached, because fear had become my daily companion. And yet, every morning, I pushed through. Not because I felt strong, but because I refused to give up.

Weekends were the only time I could breathe, and even that came with a price. I spent what little I had on hotel rooms in Newark just to be alone. Those hotel stays weren't luxury — they were survival. I needed silence. I needed space to cry, to think, to meditate, to pray, and to ask God, "Is this where my story ends, or is this the part where it shifts?"

I searched for signs — any sign — that I wasn't forgotten that there was purpose in this storm. Some weekends I found peace. Other weekends I only found more questions. But whatever I felt, it was mine. Those weekends were the only time I didn't have to perform strength for anyone.

I learned that homelessness isn't just the absence of a home — it's the absence of stability, privacy, rest, dignity, and safety. It's living in survival mode while still trying to maintain the appearance of "normal" for the world.

It's showing up to work after crying behind closed doors. It's holding on to faith when life is stripping you bare. Those nights changed me. They broke me in some ways, but they also revealed a version of myself I didn't know existed — the version that could endure pain, isolation, exhaustion, and fear, yet still show up. Still press forward. Still believe there had to be more than this.

I wasn't living; I was enduring.

But what I didn't know then was that those nights would become the blueprint for my strength — the same strength that would one day help others find their way out of the dark, too.

Seeing Homelessness Through a Human Lens – I am those lens

I know what it feels like to lose everything and still must show up like nothing is wrong. I know the shame that silence forces on you, the fear of being judged, and the exhaustion of trying to survive another day. I've crossed paths with people whose stories mirrored pieces of my own pain, and it humbled me.

Homelessness strips you down, but it also reveals truth—about people, about society, and about yourself. I share this because I've lived through storms that tried to erase me. And if you're reading this while in one of your own, I want you to know: you are not alone, and your story is not over.

Homelessness isn't one single story, it shows up differently for each person who experiences it. As I learned more and encountered people on various paths, I began to understand that losing stable housing can look many ways. Here's a more personal look at what that means:

The Five Types of Homelessness

1. When Homelessness Becomes a Long Season

Some people find themselves without a stable home for a long stretch of time—sometimes a year, sometimes longer. It often isn't because they didn't try, but because life kept handing them battles with health, trauma, or barriers that most of us never prepared for.

2. When It Happens Again and Again

There are individuals who fall in and out of homelessness at different points in their lives. It's not a lack of desire to change their circumstances—many are fighting through mental health struggles, medical challenges, or addiction, and the support they need just isn't there when they need it most.

3. When Life Turns Upside Down Overnight

For others, homelessness begins with one sudden life-changing moment: the loss of a job, a major crisis, a breakup, or something they never saw coming. They weren't always homeless—they simply ended up in a moment where life shifted faster than they could catch their footing.

4. The Homelessness No One Sees

Not everyone without a home is sleeping outside or in a shelter. Some are quietly moving from one couch to another, staying with friends or relatives, or living in overcrowded or unsafe conditions.

Their struggle is often invisible, because they're doing everything, they can to hide the shame they never deserved to feel.

5. Standing on the Edge of Losing It All

There are also people who have a roof today but know they might not have one tomorrow. They are one notice, one emergency, one paycheck away from losing everything—and there's no safety net waiting to catch them when they fall.

Surviving Homelessness

Surviving homelessness taught me the true meaning of resilience. I walked streets pretending everything was okay, but God knew the pain I carried. I learned that dignity is not found in possessions. It is found in holding on to yourself when the world tries to strip you bare. Surviving homelessness made me strong, even when I felt weak. I had to endure tests I never imagined. But through it all, I survived. I found strength in places I did not know existed. On summer nights, the heat in my van felt like a vacuum, swallowing all the air, suffocating me. The engine had to run just to stay cool enough to sleep. I survived. Resilience got me through the darkest times. I forced myself to hold my head high, even when my world felt like it was falling apart. I showed up every day. I worked hard, wearing my strength on the outside as if my life were not unraveling inside. I survived. It was not just survival instincts that kept me going. My outer appearance played the role of dignity when everything else seemed to be falling apart. At the lowest point in my life, I refused to let the world see me defeated. I survived.

Chapter 3 Workbook: Everything I Own in a Bag: Homelessness

Scripture: Isaiah 58:7 NLT

Summary:

This chapter explores the deep struggles and hidden wounds tied to this theme. It invites you to reflect honestly and discover healing through faith, resilience, and the power of second chances.

Reflection Questions:

1. How does losing stability affect you emotionally? It can be shelter, financial, emotional, mental, family, etc.

2. What gave you hope during unstable times?

Activity: Packing Light

If you had to pack five meaningful things today, what would they be and why?

Affirmation:

"I am not my past. I am my strength."

The Book of Allison: The Wounds You Don't See

Journal Space:

Chapter 4

Written By Allison K. James – Frison

Surviving the Trigger: Gun Violence

Introduction:

Although I survived the trigger, family, friends, and many from my neighborhood and surrounding areas did not.

Their faces still linger in my memory—gone too soon to violence that swallowed our streets.

Their absence weighs heavy: names continued street corners, painted in fading murals, stories that may or may not have made the newspaper.

I know some of my family members stories were never told, and their suspects were never captured.

Even now, I feel tension in my body at the sound of gunshots. My chest tightens, my breath shortens, and my mind carries me back to those moments.

The cold steel pressed against the temple of my brain was more than a weapon; it was a promise from the evil one holding the gun that my story could end right there. It stole the breath from my lungs.

I froze; my breath caught between fear and faith. I closed my eyes not knowing what my faith was then I heard a voice saying "I'm sorry" I kept my eyes closed until I knew the person was gone.

The Book of Allison: The Wounds You Don't See

Lies, Deceit, & Betrayal from "Friends"

One day I received a frantic call from Mecca a friend of mines daughter—the call started off by saying my goddaughter Puddin—was being bullied and some girls wanted to fight her. Me and three other friends of mine, Red, Me-Me and Gee-Gee drove to where they were to help. As soon as we hopped out of the car, ready to defend my goddaughter, Puddin the alleged bullies ambushed us. They were waiting for us—with bats, knives, and guns. It was too late to get back into the car; we were surrounded.

All we could do was fight for our lives and hope we made it out of there alive. As we tried to escape, I could not find my car keys. While I was searching, a man sneaked up behind me and hit me in the face with the butt of his gun while I am sitting in the car. Eventually someone threw the car keys to us, and we pulled off—just as the same man started shooting at us while we were trying to escape. No one was shot; however, I learned that the person's name was Bully, growing up in Newark, especially in the projects everyone had a nickname.

I drove straight to the hospital. I was examined and all results were fine. However, the side of my life face was swollen, I had bandages on my face and an ice pack pressed to my bruises. We all survived and that was the last time I ever ran into a fight to defend against anyone, we all could have lost our lives that evening.

Later I learned the truth: my so-called friend Mecca had lied. They were not there to defend their daughter; they were setting us up. While we fought, she did nothing. We could have been killed. I never forgave her for putting me and my friends in that situation.

When I went to my annual visit with my Optometrist, I learned that I was left with a permanent scar insider my left eye from being hit with the butt of that pistol.

#DearGod #ThankYou

The Hand That Held the Trigger — I Call Him Jesus: The Elevator Stop

It was a cold winter day. I had just gotten off work and decided to stop by my friend Paw's apartment in the projects. When I pulled into the parking lot, it was unusually empty. As I walked toward the building, I heard a voice I recognized calling my name, but I ignored it—I did not want to talk. Suddenly someone came hurrying toward me. Before I could react, she grabbed me by the neck, pressed a gun to my head, and forced me into the elevator. Inside, she jammed the door between two floors so no one could get in or out. She pressed the iron of the gun against my temple and demanded everything I had she was robbing me, I told her I had nothing, my purse was in the car.

She pressed the gun harder while saying I'm going to blow your brains out if you don't give me what I want. I repeated that "I don't have nothing; my purse is in my car." At that moment she pulled the trigger. The gun jammed, God intervened. She sad I'm sorry and ran out of the elevator. I released the biggest exhale with tears storming down my face. I did not know whether to ride the elevator up or down or go to Paw's apartment. My feet, frozen with fear, wedged the door. Finally, I rode down.

#DearGod #ThankYou

When the elevator door opened, I gasped for air, not realizing I had been holding my breath—only to be met by a sea of blue uniforms, guns drawn and pointed directly at me.

The Book of Allison: The Wounds You Don't See

Within seconds, I was rushed outside by Police Officers, placed in the back of a police squad car, and taken to a makeshift community police station. They questioned me for hours—no food, no water, no phone call. All they wanted was my statement.

After hours of interrogation, an officer finally told me I was free to go. Free? The suspect was still out there, and yet no one offered me a ride home.

No one asked if I was okay or needed anything. They gave me no resources, no next steps, just a cold dismissal, as if I were the one who had committed a crime.

Returning to the projects after all that felt surreal. I was greeted with cheers, like a hero. Neighbors welcomed me as if I was a celebrity. That moment forced me to realize how survival had become a badge of honor in our community. Gun violence had become so common in subsidized housing that trauma felt normalized.

When gunshots rang out, we ducked or ran into the nearest building—but within minutes we were back outside, jumping rope, playing with rocks and glass, tossing a football, or just sitting outside, laughing, and joking like nothing had just happened.

Eddie: My Soulmate

God works in mysterious ways. Eddie and I were on a break, but I found myself missing him. At 3 AM, I called him, asking what he was doing. He was cooking, so I invited him over to the room I was renting, and we stayed up all night talking and listening to music holding each other and stirring into each other's eyes. The next morning, I got up and prepared myself for work. Eddie was still asleep, so I kissed him on the cheek and left.

As I walked to the bus stop, a strong feeling came over me. Without thinking, I did an about-face and headed back to the house. I went inside, opened the bedroom door, and said, "Eddie, I hope you can hear me, I love you." Then I left again and went to work.

At work, I called him repeatedly, but there was no answer. I decided to call his cousin to see if he had heard from him. He said, "Yes, I believe he's on his way back home." When my friend Mary picked me up from work, I immediately began paging him when I got home, but still no response. Finally, my phone started ringing and I noticed it was a number from a payphone that everyone used in the projects. I was excited, smiling, thinking it was him.

However, it was Beat calling one of his friends. I knew something was wrong because Beat voice was low and shaking. I was not prepared for that phone call. Beat muffed Eddie had just been shot by a police officer.

I remember that phone call like it was yesterday. I recall saying to myself "I know Eddie was not out there having a shootout with the police, and why would the police be shooting at him." I froze. My brain felt like it was in a fog, and everything the caller said sounded muffled.

The only words that stood out were, "It doesn't look good for him." I do not remember the call ending, but what I do remember is the feeling I had earlier that morning before work, it re-entered my body, and I became numb with fear.

I headed to the bathroom to change my clothes when my phone rang again. Mary answered it, and I passed out. It was like my soul had left my body and, Eddie last breath was through me. I knew at that moment that Eddie had taken his last breath. When I regained consciousness, Mary was still on the phone. It was Eddie's cousin, Dimples, I told Mary to let her know: "I know Eddie just died his soul passed through me, when he took his last breath, I felt it."

There were many stories about what happened that day. Some said he was shot by the police officers during a shootout; others claimed it was someone seeking revenge for the day before. Whatever the truth, the fact remained that he was shot several times at the baseball field on Howard Street.

On the day of Eddie's funeral, I noticed something strange: tears were streaming down his face. I remember asking someone else if they saw it, and they confirmed it. A few days after his funeral, I had a dream. He was sitting on my doorstep at the house I was renting, where our last physical encounter took place, in the same clothes he wore when he got shot. He asked me one question: "Why did you let them bury me alive?"

I never answered him, but I kept shouting, "What happened? What happened?" because I had heard so many different versions of the story. I needed to hear it from him. But he never answered. All he would say was, "Why did you let them bury me alive?" I had no answer for him he was pronounced unalive at the hospital and out of fear I never went to the morgue, I refused to see him in that image.

I wanted my last memory of us together to be of that night. We held each other tight, staring in each other's eyes, while listening to music.

I often wondered if he made it to heaven. I dreamed about him a lot, and in one of those dreams, he kept saying, "I have a surprise for you." I watched as he pushed someone toward me. As they got closer, I realized that someone was my mother. He was pushing her in a wheelchair, and at that moment, I knew—he made it to heaven, I was able to exhale.

#DearGod #ThankYou

My Heart Still Beats for My Brother Spencer, Jr.

Now, you all remember when I said that my brother Spencer was strong as an elephant, right? I can remember when I was young, I had to be about ten years old. My sisters, the ones that were still living at home, and we were woken by the sound of our front door being slammed and my brother's bedroom door slamming.

My mother jumped out of her bed and walked swiftly to my brother's bedroom, that's when we all jumped out of bed and peeked down the hallway to where my brother's room was. I heard my mother ask, "what is wrong with you, why are you slamming doors in my house." He responded by saying "I was shot four times in my chest." My mother screaming and with fear in her voice told him to get up out of bed and come into the hallway so she could look at him.

When he came out of the bedroom, my eyes widened, I could see blood all over his shirt and pants. He sat down in a chair like nothing was wrong. Spencer ran from wherever he was with four bullet wounds in his chest.

The Book of Allison: The Wounds You Don't See

My mother called EMS, when they arrived there were several police officers with them. I was scared and started crying, that was the first time I saw someone shot in person, usually I would see people on television or in the movies getting shot. I never thought that I would experience it in real life, especially someone in my own family. Spencer was taken to the hospital and I never seen him again for the next three years or so.

As I am typing this portion of my book, I can see as clear as day; the day it happened. I can see the little girl in me peeking out of her bedroom door, eyes wide open, wearing a pink gown with tears in her eyes. I can see my mother and brother sitting together waiting for the EMS to arrive. I see myself looking out of my bedroom window watching four police cars in the parking lot with lights on, my brother being rolled out of the building into the back of the EMS truck with my mother behind them trying her best to be strong, wiping tears from her eyes while looking up to our bedroom window to see if we can see her. Although he survived those memories will always be part of the wounds you don't see.

The Call: "Auntie, Uncle was Shot."

The call I received felt surreal. I could not fully process the information at first, so I did what anyone would do in shock—I attempted to go back to sleep, hoping it was just a nightmare. But my phone rang again, and the voice on the other end hit me like a punch to the gut. My brother had been shot in the head, and I needed to get to the hospital. The news felt like a bad dream, but it was not. It was reality. I could not understand how this was possible.

My brother was the one who cracked jokes with everyone, a carefree spirit who never messed with anyone. He loved to dance and sing and make sure everyone was safe. How could something like this happen to him?

With trembling hands, I slowly forced myself out of bed, shaking, holding my knees to keep myself from falling. I thought, just maybe, if I drove slowly enough, the story might change by the time I arrived. The streets blurred as I drove, my head spinning with questions, my pulse racing faster than my car and my heart skipping beats as the panic would not disappear.

When I arrived at the hospital, the sharp, sterile smell of antiseptic hit me like a slap in the face. Detectives stood off to the side, and I realized that this was not a bad dream, or a nightmare I could not wake up from.

The waiting room was filled with family members and friends, their worried faces reflecting the weight of the same grim reality. The hospital policy only allowed two visitors at a time, but I sneaked in to see my brother, hoping my presence might offer him something more than just my silent prayers.

The sight of him lying there, motionless, was enough to steal my breath. He was still fully clothed, but there was too much blood. The room smelled of antiseptics and something sharper, something colder. No one was working on him. No one was trying to stop the bleeding. No one seemed to care. I felt my heart race, my hands shaking as I rushed to the nurses' station. "Why hasn't anyone been in to help him?" I demanded.

The response was cold: they were waiting for the neurosurgeon to arrive and the supervisor in charge of the emergency room that night.

The Book of Allison: The Wounds You Don't See

I yelled "What the fuck do you mean you are waiting for someone, my brother is bleeding, he has a bullet hole in his head, he need help now, he needs to be cleaned up, nobody wants to see their loved one laying in a sea of blood."

The nurse got up off her ass and gather some supplies, while asking me to go back into the waiting room, of course, I did not.

I refused to leave. I had heard that if you talk to someone in a state like that, they might hear you—so I sang, knowing it was the worst rendition of a song he had ever heard. "Ain't no mountain high enough," I sang, my voice cracking under the pressure. But as I sang, his leg twitched. His hand moved. And even though one of his eyes was closed, the other blinked. That small movement was enough to reignite my hope.

I ran out of the room, shouting, "He is moving! He is not dead!" I rushed back to his bedside, calling his name repeatedly, desperately waiting for him to respond. Finally, the neurosurgeon and neurologists arrived, along with a few nurses. They told us that his condition was dire, and the situation was worse than we could imagine. But they promised they would do their best.

A few days later, we were called to a family meeting. I already knew what that meant: it was never a good sign. We were told that we needed to decide whether we wanted them to operate. The doctor laid it out bluntly: if we did not operate, he would die. But if they did, there was no guarantee he would survive. Even if he did survive, they warned, they did not know what his life would look like afterward. They explained that depending on what part of the brain had been damaged, he might never remember anything. I remember me and my siblings looking at my father's sister Aunt Mae. She was the aunt that we called on for guidance whenever we were in a family emergency, and she would relate the news to the rest of my father's siblings.

Aunt Mae told us "This is your brother, and you all have to decide what you think is best for your brother." I stated we cannot sit around and do nothing, we all decided to have the surgery, the experts stated if we did nothing my brother would die, I played that in my head over and over.

We decided to go ahead with the surgery. The next seven hours felt like an eternity. It was the longest stretch of time I had ever endured. Although the surgery was a success, they placed him in an induced coma to reduce activity in his brain. We took shifts, staying at the hospital around the clock in case he woke up. But when I asked the surgeon when they would take my brother out of the coma, his answer left me stunned: "We decided medically to place your brother in a coma, but it's up to him to come out on his own and the brain has a mind of its own."

The words crushed me. I had always believed in faith, but I had lost it over the years. But this time, I prayed—not for myself, but for him. I had to. When I got home, I planned on kneeling down to pray; however, I found myself lying on the floor, unsure of what to say.

But my words came out, raw and desperate. "God, you have taken my mother, my father, and my fiancé. Now you are coming for my siblings. I cannot take another loss. Just tell me what it is you need me to do, and I will do it. Please, spare my brother's life. Let him breathe again."

The next day, I arrived at the hospital with my sister Shelva, my second mom, who was a nurse, and I could barely contain my excitement when Shelva told me that our brother was breathing on his own. Spencer's assigned nurse was in the room, I was waiting for him to say she was lying; however, those words never came out of his mouth.

The Book of Allison: The Wounds You Don't See

I looked at the nurse and said he looked like himself again, you cannot tell he had any injury to his brain. What Spencer's assigned nurse told me those words stuck with me, something I will never forget: "It is not what you see on the outside that matters. It is what is going on inside of him—the wounds you cannot see—that matter most." That hit home for me because I was living that life. What you see is not always what you get. However, I knew the conversation I had with my God the night before.

His head was swollen, the size of a watermelon. But that morning, the swelling had gone down. His skin was glowing, smooth, as though he had not been shot in the head. The only sign of the trauma was the bandages wrapped around his head. It felt like a miracle. I could not believe what I was seeing.

After my conversation with God, things began to move quickly. Within three weeks, my brother was transferred from the CICU to the ICU, and then to a regular hospital room. But he had to have a tracheotomy to help him breathe. I could not believe how quickly he recovered. But I always remember that conversation, I had with God on my bedroom floor.

While my brother was healing so was I. One night, when I got home, something inside me snapped. I poured out every drop of alcohol I had; the bar was no longer a part of my home décor. I did not go to rehab; I did not join a program; I had no sponsor—I just knew I wanted something better for myself, and God was working on me. And for the last twenty years, I have been sober.

A few days later, I received a call from my brother's social worker telling me he would be moved to a Rehabilitation Center. I immediately refused. "He's not ready to leave the hospital!" I insisted.

But she explained that he was being moved that day, and she asked if I wanted to ride with him or follow the transportation van.

I was so upset that I threatened to go there and kick her ass, but she hung up on me. That call triggered something deep within me. I called my sister Zanna she had a copy of my apartment keys. I told her to grab a signed check from my desk—just in case I needed to be bailed out. I told her my plans, and she laughed. However, I was dead ass serious.

By the time I arrived, my brother had already been transported. I was beyond furious, but I knew I could not let it take my focus away from him.

At the rehabilitation center, we took turns visiting him, my sisters and I all had a day to visit. On Wednesdays, I would always go. I made it to a point to stop at the nurses' station first to get an update to see how Spencer, Jr. was doing. During one visit, the nurse told me, "You can ask him yourself. After six months, his tracheotomy was removed today."

My heart dropped. I was both terrified and hopeful, what if he did not remember me? What if he did not know who I was? When I entered his room, he was staring out the window. I stayed by the door, still unsure of what to expect. I called his name softly and asked him. "Do you know who I am?" I asked.

He did not turn my way; however, he answered, "Yes, my sister Al-nisa." Al-nisa was the Muslim name he gave me when I was a teenager, all his sisters had Mulsim names when we were younger; however, he never stopped calling us by those names.

"How did you know it was me without turning around?" I asked, my voice trembling.

He smiled and said, "I can see your face through the window."

Tears flooded my eyes, and I walked over to him, holding his hand. "Do you want anything?" I asked.

He looked at me and said, "Yes, ice cream."

My tears turned into laughter, and for the next thirty minutes, we held hands and watched TV together. It was one of the happiest moments of my life.

As I left the hospital, I had a "Jesus moment" in the elevator. I was crying and shouting, "Thank you, Jesus!" I skipped to my car, feeling lighter than I had in years. As he healed, so did my faith.

After the surgery, the tracheotomy, and months of rehab, my brother had permanent short-term memory loss, partial paralysis on his right side, and blindness in his right eye—the side on which he was shot.

But we accepted it. He was alive. We were thankful that he was not shot on his left side, as he was left-handed, and that is where all his strength lay.

He spent the next 13 years living with these challenges, and we continued to walk on eggshells every time he went to the hospital, wondering if this were the day God would call him home. But we knew this: our thoughts are not God's thoughts.

When COVID swept through the world, my brother was living in a nursing home. And in the end, he passed away due to complications, just as so many others did in nursing homes during that time.

The pain of losing him took pieces of my heart I did not even know were missing. Pain became my silent partner, but even in that, I knew he was at peace.

During that time going home services were not the same. I felt bad for my brother, which was the loneliness of the home service I had attended in my life.

Only three family members were allowed to attend the cemetery by the time we arrived they were already placing him in his grave, and the family could not get out of the car. My immediate household members and I sat in the car. I said a prayer and sang a song letting him know that we were there.

On his one-year anniversary my family and I went to visit him. We could not find his resting place. I learned that doing the pandemic, funeral homes and cemeteries were stretched thin and, it appeared that they could not keep up with labeling the gravesites.

We stood in the middle of the cemetery, prayed, cried, and released balloons in remembrance of our beloved brother, Spencer L. James, Jr.

#TheWoundsYouDontSee

Chapter 4 Workbook: Surviving the Trigger: Gun Violence

Scripture: Romans 8:18 NIV

Summary:

This chapter explores the deep struggles and hidden wounds tied to this theme. It invites you to reflect honestly and discover healing through faith, resilience, and the power of second chances.

Reflection Questions:

1. What triggers remind you of your past trauma?

_____
_____
_____
_____

2. What strategies help you cope when you feel unsafe?

_____
_____
_____
_____

Activity: Trigger Tracker

Identify three common triggers and write two healthy responses for each.

_____
_____
_____
_____
_____
_____
_____

Affirmation:

"I am not my past. I am my strength."

Journal Space:

_____
_____
_____
_____
_____
_____
_____
_____
_____
_____
_____
_____

The Book of Allison: The Wounds You Don't See

Chapter 5

Written By Allison K. James – Frison

Trauma & Child Abuse - Breaking the Silence

Introduction:

Not all wounds can be seen. Some live deep inside, hidden behind our smiles, laughter, silence, and the way we move through the world.

Trauma and abuse leave scars on the heart that can feel impossible to heal. But even in those dark places, there is light. I saw the light. I am living through the light. And I am the light.

This chapter is not here to reopen old wounds, but to remind you that your story does not end with pain. You are more than what happened to you, and you are victorious. Healing is not instant, and it does not erase the past—but with faith, courage, and safe spaces, it transforms the way we carry it.

As you walk through these pages, give yourself permission to be honest with your feelings, gentle with your heart, and open to the truth that God has always been close to you—even in the hardest moments.

You are not broken beyond repair. You are loved, you are seen, and you are healing, one step at a time.

Trauma

I remember the day my dad left the house on October 17, 1987. He said he was going to a friend's house to watch the football game. That was the last day I saw my father alive.

The story I was told—though it does not erase the pain—was that my dad was at his friend's house, where two brothers lived, and their sister was there. She started an argument with my father. He ignored her, but she became so angry that she knocked his plate of food off the table. One of the brothers tried to fix him on another plate, but when he returned, she grabbed a knife and stabbed my father in the chest.

I can only imagine the chaos, the panic, the fear that must have seized my dad as he realized his life was slipping away. He ran out of the house, collapsed across the street in front of a store, and was pronounced unalive on the scene.

This day will forever be etched in my heart as it broke into a million pieces. I would not wish this on anyone.

My dad was the first man who loved me, and he was the first man I loved. The nicknames he gave me, the way he called me "Princess" or "Duke"—I would never hear them again. My life, and part of my heart, was taken from me in an instant. I had just graduated high school, trying to figure out how I was going to go to college, and suddenly, she robbed me of the chance to share my successes with the person who believed in me the most.

I decided to delay college. I was traumatized, timid, and only felt safe around family and friends. What was supposed to be a short break turned into thirty years before I eventually went to college to achieve what I knew my parents would be proud of.

Everyone manages trauma differently, but for me, I became a bully. The 10-year-old girl inside me re-emerged, angry and hurt. But this was not just a temporary loss. I could never go back to those moments, never hear my father's voice again.

He was taken from me by someone's anger, intoxicated emotions with mental health illness, someone's senseless violence. And that is what still stings the most: his life was stolen in a moment of foolishness and fury.

My father's death is a truth that still feels too heavy to hold. One minute, he was a part of my world, and the next, he was gone—ripped away by a cruelty I will never understand.

The violence did not just take his life; it shattered mine. His absence is more than just missing someone. It is a wound you cannot see but feel in the depths of your soul. His children were left without a father, we were fatherless.

The Day Justice Was Served.

The day of the hearing was Thursday, March 2, 1989, all my father's children were there along with my aunties and uncle. I did not know what was going on, I was seventeen years old and had no knowledge of the terminology the Judge, Public Defendant or Prosecutor was saying. All I can remember is that Melissa was giving a plea bargain.

However, she was found guilty of manslaughter because she was intoxicated and the prosecutor that was overseeing the case learned that Melissa had also stabbed someone else out of state and was intoxicated during that incident as well.

The Book of Allison: The Wounds You Don't See

Melissa was found guilty of manslaughter and was sentenced to ten years in prison and was ordered to receive substance abuse treatment while in prison.

Thirty-eight years later, I still have the news article from that court hearing.

The headline read:

"Victim's family gets maximum for killer." The word killer wounded my soul like a knife was engraved into my heart.

"When the police arrived, Melissa was obviously under the influence of alcohol, the officer told the court. He said she initially slapped James and threw his food on the floor. When her sister's boyfriend gave James a new dish, Natalie slapped him again and then got a kitchen knife and stabbed James, said the assistant prosecutor. James ran out of the house and collapsed across the street from the house; he was pronounced unlived at the scene of the crime."

My father was a good man, he did not believe in hitting women; however, when I read the news article, I told myself "I wish my father would have bet the shit out her maybe he would still be alive."

About twenty years later my organization Girls Live, Love, Laugh Inc. hosted our first Community Thanksgiving Dinner at my Church. I was helping my mentees make plates to serve the senior citizens. I turned around and there she was Melissa. I froze, she was much older and looked like life was rough for her; however, I was 100% sure that it was her. I stood there looking at her for some time asking myself what I should do. I walked over to her and asked if she knew anyone named Spencer James or DOC, his nickname.

She never turned to look at me in my face; however, she shook her head no. I took a picture of her; however, it was only the side of her face because she would not look up. I sent the picture to my sibling to see if it were indeed her; however, they could not tell because her face was down. I knew it was her.

I will never forget her face of the woman who took my father's life. And, I still have that picture of her from that day, why, I do not know. That day, I opened closed wounds, who would have thought that I would run into the person who stole my father's life and left his children fatherless.

Intro to Childhood Silence

My childhood memories are fragmented, scattered like pieces of a puzzle I cannot quite put together. For years, silence was my way of coping with pain, until a moment in my forties forced the past to surface.

What began with a surgeon's question became my first step toward breaking free. She asked if I had ever experienced childhood abuse, and I could only remember one name—Skye.

Though the details remain unclear, speaking my truth became the doorway to healing. Today, I mentor young girls, around the same age when my own voice was silenced, reminding them—and myself—that their voices deserve to be heard. I hope to ignite positive change and a brighter future for all the Allison's of the world.

The Book of Allison: The Wounds You Don't See

Child Abuse

My childhood was far from the sanctuary it should have been. It was stolen, piece by piece. Betrayal planted seeds of silence that grew into forests of shame. I was ten years old when the trauma started. I often wonder why my memory is so limited when it comes to those early years. It is like those moments are behind a locked door, one that only creaks open at times, letting out fragments of things I cannot fully piece together.

It took me years—decades even—to realize that what happened to me was not my fault, and that my voice was not broken, only buried.

The door to those memories started to nudge open during an emergency surgery in my forties. The surgeon, while examining me, asked, "Did you ever experience childhood abuse?" She had noticed scar tissue and, with her years of practice, recognized its meaning.

Her question startled me. Though I said "no" without hesitation, my mind started racing, trying to figure out why I had unexplained scars.

As a child, I had a stutter, and I was given speech therapy in school to help me speak more clearly. For years, I thought I had overcome it, but suddenly, my old stutter returned. It was as if the 10-year-old younger me had resurfaced, trembling and afraid to speak.

For so many years, silence had been my shield. I never told anyone about the abuse—not out of mistrust or lack of love, but because the words were too heavy, too confusing. Abuse has a way of tying knots around your tongue and locking memories away.

But after that surgery, something shifted. It was the fragility of life that surgery reminded me of, or it was the return of my child's voice, but I knew I could no longer carry this secret alone.

Breaking the Silence

When I returned to my sister Jackie's house to recover, surrounded by family, I knew it was time. I asked my siblings if they knew anyone named Skye. The room went still. They exchanged confused looks, shaking their heads. To them, the name meant nothing. To me, it was the only piece of the puzzle I had. The name my abuser had given me.

That moment—both liberating and heartbreaking—was the beginning of my healing. I could no longer hide my truth. It was not about remembering every detail. It was about letting go of the silence.

Afterward, my siblings began asking questions, but there were no answers. They wanted to know who had hurt me, but all I had was the name Skye and a vague image in my mind. They struggled to understand how this could have happened without their knowledge, but I could not offer them more than what I had.

What I learned, and what I want to share with you, is this: silence protects no one. For years, I thought burying my pain would make it disappear, but pain that is buried alive does not die. It waits. And it shows itself in diverse ways—through anxiety, fear, and fragmented memories.

Breaking my silence was my first step toward healing. Even though my words were incomplete, I no longer felt trapped by them. I never looked into therapy; however, during Covid-19 after the loss of my brother and my sister being in a coma, I knew at that moment therapy was necessary for me to live with the current and past trauma I endured.

To my surprise speaking to someone really helped and not to mention my therapist allowed me to have control of the session. I talked, she listened and at the end of each session she would give me coping skills to try and encourage me to spend more time with myself and focus on Allison. After six-eight months, we agreed that these sessions were no longer needed, and I could text/call her whenever I felt I needed a session with her.

Redemption and Healing

I now mentor young girls. I see myself in them, their innocence, their curiosity, their need to be seen and heard. When I sit with them, I am reminded that their voices matter, and they deserve to be protected. I show up for them because I know what it is like to be silent.

Each conversation I have is an act of redemption—not only for them, but for my younger self. Every time I remind a girl that she is worthy, I am healing a little more. And every time I advocate for a child in need, I am helping to break the silence that has haunted me for so long.

I am who I am today because of what I have gone through. My trauma, my pain, my resilience have shaped me into the strong, empathetic, determined person I am now. I am a helper, a social worker, and most importantly, I am a child of God. Every action I take is driven by the purpose that was born from my past.

To my fellow sisters, and brothers I cannot continue to say this YOU ARE NOT ALONE. Share your truth and shame the devil. Healing begins with you.

I am not broken. I am a survivor, and I have chosen to be the light.

Chapter 5 Workbook: Trauma & Child Abuse

Scripture: Romans 8:18 NIV

Summary:

This chapter defines trauma as the emotional and psychological response to events that overwhelm an individual's ability to cope. It can stem from a wide range of experiences, including accidents, violence, natural disasters, or loss. It invites you to reflect honestly and discover healing through faith, resilience, and the power of second chances.

Reflection Questions:

1. What feelings do you carry from painful experiences?
   _____
   _____
   _____
   _____

2. Who are the safest people you can talk to when you feel uncomfortable?
   _____
   _____
   _____
   _____

3. How has God shown you comfort in challenging times?
   _____
   _____
   _____
   _____

The Book of Allison: The Wounds You Don't See

Activity: My Safe Space

Describe a place (real or imagined) where you feel completely safe, loved, and protected. Add details about the sights, sounds, and feelings in that space.

_____
_____
_____
_____
_____
_____
_____
_____
_____
_____
_____
_____

Repeat after me:

I am worthy of love, healing, and peace.

Journal Space:

_____
_____
_____
_____
_____
_____
_____
_____
_____
_____
_____
_____

Chapter 6

Written by Allison K. James – Frison

I'm Still Smart — I Just Learn Differently

Education

For forty-nine years, no one saw me for whom I truly was—not even me. I had a learning disability. Education is supposed to empower every child to thrive, but sometimes policies and systems often fail to see the individual behind the grades. I experienced this firsthand. Speech therapy was my only support, and yet I went from kindergarten through high school with undiagnosed learning disabilities.

My mentees inspired me to return to school. I asked them about their future plans, most of them wanted to go to college. That's when I realized I had no college experience to advise them; I enrolled at forty-seven years old. I failed and retook classes, eventually excelling, yet still unaware that my lifelong struggles were tied to a learning disability. However, I graduated with honors at Essex County College.

At 49, I finally received a formal evaluation and discovered I had a learning disability my entire life unrecognized because I was compliant, quiet, and diligent. My experience is far from unique. Across the country, children are unseen, unevaluated, and unsupported. Decisions made by leaders often determine who gets help and who falls through the cracks.

Education is political. Policy shapes opportunity, recognition, and empowerment. Funding disparities, standardized testing, and lack of support create invisible barriers. Advocacy, early identification, and inclusive teaching practices are essential to ensure no child is left behind. My story is both proof of the problem and a blueprint for change.

Education is more than a system; it is a lifeline. Politics shapes every strand of that lifeline. By advocating, mentoring, and raising awareness, we can ensure children are seen, supported, and empowered. This is why I ran for office—and became the Vice President of a public school who publicly speaks about her learning disability and advocate for our special needs students to ensure fair opportunities and access to resources as their peers. But beyond politics and policy, we must remember what is at stake: a child's belief in themselves.

Every child deserves more than a seat in a classroom—they deserve a space where they feel safe, heard, and valued. A healthy learning environment is not just about clean buildings and good lighting, it is about the emotional and psychological safety that allows a child to take academic risks, ask questions, and be vulnerable without shame. It is about educators having training and time to recognize when a student is struggling—not just academically, but emotionally or socially.

I learned late in life that you can appear "fine" on the outside and still be drowning inside. Many children walk that same tightrope every day. They smile, stay quiet, do what is expected—but inside, they try to survive school instead of thriving in it. That is not education. That is endurance. True equity in education means acknowledging that every child's path is different. It means providing not just resources, but relationships—trusted adults who see them, advocate for them, and believe in their potential.

It means making space for neurodiversity, cultural identity, and lived experience inside the classroom—not just in theory, but in practice.

When we provide children with a healthy and safe environment, we give them permission to be themselves. We show them they are not broken, they just learn differently. And that is not a flaw; it is a strength.

The future of education must be personal, not always political. It must be about the child in front of us, not just the policies above us. Because when we center children, their dignity, their well-being, their full humanity—we do not just build better schools. We build a better world.

Chapter: 6 Workbook: I am Still Smart, I Just Learn Differently: Education & Politics

Scripture: Proverbs 1:7 NIV

Summary:

This chapter explores the deep struggles and hidden wounds tied to this theme. It invites you to reflect honestly and discover healing through faith, resilience, and the power of second chances.

Reflection Questions:

1. How has education shaped your journey?

_____
_____
_____
_____
_____
_____
_____

2. What challenges or barriers have you faced in learning?

_____
_____
_____
_____
_____
_____
_____

The Book of Allison: The Wounds You Don't See

Activity: Strengths Map

List five unique strengths or talents you have, beyond academics.

1,

2.

3.

4.

5.

Affirmation:

"I am not my past. I am my strength."

Journal Space:

_____
_____
_____
_____
_____
_____
_____
_____
_____
_____
_____
_____

Chapter 7

Written By Allison K. James – Frison

The Voices of Girls Matter

Introduction:

Every wound carries a story, but every story also carries the potential for purpose. Out of my journey through pain and healing, a vision was born—a vision to create something greater than myself, something that could pour into the lives of young girls the way I once wished someone had poured into me. That vision became Girls Live, Love, Laugh Inc.

I created this nonprofit organization because I believe with all my heart that the voices of girls matter. That their education matters. That their image matters. That their representation matters. And above all, their future matters. Too often, society tries to silence or minimize the voices of girls, especially those from underserved communities. But when you silence a girl, you silence a future leader, a dreamer, a creator, or a girl that can change the world.

Through mentorship, encouragement, and empowerment, Girls Live, Love, Laugh Inc. is dedicated to helping girls become the best version of themselves. It is not just about programs or activities, it is about planting seeds of confidence, resilience, and self-worth that will grow with them for a lifetime.

My upbringing shaped the heart of this organization. I know what it feels like to be overlooked, to feel unseen, and to carry struggles in silence.

But I also know what it means to rise above those challenges. I use my story to remind each girl that no matter where she starts, she has the power to beat the odds.

When a girl learns to live with purpose, love herself fully, and laugh through life's storms, she becomes unstoppable. She begins to see that her circumstances do not define her vision, her strength, and her determination do.

But it does not stop there. My hope is not just to inspire confidence, but to train girls to walk boldly into every room knowing their worth, to carry themselves with dignity, and to lead without apology. They should be taught that it is okay to take up space, speak up, and stand tall—but to do so with grace, kindness, and respect. We do not just raise voices, we raise values.

To live without regrets means encouraging girls to make decisions rooted in self-respect and long-term vision. It means teaching them that their bodies, minds, and hearts are sacred—and that they never have to trade pieces of themselves to be accepted. Mistakes will happen, but when girls are equipped with strong mentors and a solid moral compass, they learn to grow from those moments instead of being defined by them.

To love on purpose is to love intentionally—not just romantically, but in all relationships, starting with self-love. We teach girls to set boundaries, to surround themselves with people who uplift them, and to pursue goals that align with their purpose. Purposeful love is empowering love—it is not rooted in validation but in value.

And we teach them to laugh aloud—not just quietly in the corner, but boldly and joyfully, even when life is hard. Laughter is healing. Joy is revolutionary. In a world that often asks women to be quiet, small, or serious, we remind girls that their joy is not only welcome—it is necessary.

Most importantly, we show them how to be bold yet respectful. Being bold does not mean being loud for attention, it means being courageous in conviction. It means speaking truth with love, standing up for others, and knowing when to lead and when to listen. Respect is not weakness; it is wisdom.

Girls Live, Love, Laugh Inc. is more than a nonprofit. It is a movement. It is a promise to every young girl that she is worthy, that she belongs, and that her future is limitless. My hope is that through this program, generations of girls will rise—stronger, bolder, and ready to take their place in the world as leaders, innovators, and women who believe in themselves.

This chapter of my life is not just about surviving my own wounds; it is about helping others discover that their lives have meaning too. The greatest gift I can give back to the world is to ensure that no girl ever doubts that her story, her dreams, and her future matter.

Because when a girl knows her worth, she becomes unstoppable.

Chapter 7 Workbook: The Voices of Girls Matter: Identity and Self-Worth

For Women Committed to Living Without Regret, Loving on Purpose, and Leading Boldly

Introduction:

This Work is Sacred

This chapter is more than a story—it is a call to action. As women, we carry generations of silence, sacrifice, strength, and survival. Some of us are just now learning to speak up. Some of us are still healing from what we were taught to suppress.

And many of us are determined to raise up a generation of girls who know their worth early—before the world teaches them to forget.

This workbook is your space to reflect, restore, and realign. Whether you are a mentor, a mother, an educator, or simply a woman on her own healing journey—you are the message. The way you live, love, and lead creates a blueprint for the girls who follow.

Section One: Live Without Regret

"I will no longer shrink to make others comfortable. I choose to live fully, with intention, and without apology."

The Book of Allison: The Wounds You Don't See

Journal Prompt:

1. Where in your life have you settled when you were meant to soar?

   _____
   _____
   _____
   _____
   _____
   _____
   _____
   _____
   _____
   _____
   _____
   _____

2. What would it look like to live without regrets starting today?

   _____
   _____
   _____
   _____
   _____
   _____
   _____
   _____
   _____
   _____
   _____
   _____
   _____

Write freely:

The Book of Allison: The Wounds You Don't See

Reflection Exercise: The "Yes" & "No" List

Draw two columns. In the left, write five things you are saying YES to (joy, boundaries, growth). In the right, write five things you are releasing or saying NO to (guilt, fear, people-pleasing).

YES To: NO To:

Example: My authentic voice
Example: Shrinking myself

Section Two: Love On Purpose

"Self-love isn't selfish. It's the foundation of every healthy relationship you'll ever have."

Journal Prompt:

What kind of love have you been modeling—for your daughter, your mentee, or even yourself?

_____
_____
_____
_____

The Book of Allison: The Wounds You Don't See

What would change if you loved yourself on purpose every day?

Write Honestly:

Healing Letter Exercise: Write to the Girl You Once Were

Write a letter to your younger self, the girl who needed to hear that she was enough.

Start with:

"Dear Younger, Me, I want you to know..."

_____
_____
_____
_____
_____
_____
_____
_____
_____
_____
_____
_____
_____
_____
_____
_____
_____
_____
_____
_____
_____
_____
_____
_____
_____

The Book of Allison: The Wounds You Don't See

Section Three: Laugh Out Loud

"Your joy is not a luxury. It's a revolutionary act of resistance and healing."

Joy Inventory:

Write three things that bring you deep, genuine joy, then plan to experience at least one of them in the next 7 days.

1.
2.
3.

Plan your joy moment:

"I will give myself permission to _____ by _____."

Section Four: Be Bold, Be Respectful

"Boldness is not aggression. Boldness is rooted in clarity, purpose, and self-respect."

Journal Prompt:

When was the last time you dimmed your light to make others comfortable?

What would it look like to walk boldly in your truth, while staying grounded in grace?

Reflect:

Identity Statement:

Craft a powerful "I Am" statement that reflects who you are becoming.

Example:

I am a woman of faith and fire.

I speak truth with love.

I lead with humility and power.

Now write your own:

"I am..."

_____
_____
_____
_____

The Book of Allison: The Wounds You Don't See

Section Five: She Rises

"You are raising a generation—not just of girls, but of women who will change the world."

Mentorship Reflection:

Who is watching you, learning from you, and being impacted by your example?

What legacy do you want to leave in the lives of the girls you influence?

Write your legacy vision:

Final Reflection: Becoming Her

Close your workbook by completing the sentence below:

"The best version of myself is a woman who..."

_____
_____
_____
_____
_____
_____

_____
_____
_____
_____
_____
_____
_____
_____
_____
_____

Closing Words:

You are the message before you ever say a word.

The girls you mentor, raise, or influence will become what you reflect:

A woman who lives boldly, loves with intention, and laughs aloud—without regret.

Keep becoming her. She is powerful. She is necessary.

And she is you.

You do not need to have every answer today. You do not need to have your path mapped out perfectly. Growth is not about perfection — it is about presence. It is about showing up for the version of yourself that is trying to emerge, even when you feel unsure.

Every time you choose to love yourself, even a little.

Every time you tell the truth, even when your voice shakes.

Every time you choose healing instead of hiding.

Every time you stand back up after life knocks you down —you are becoming her.

The world has enough people pretending.

What the world needs is your light.

Your realness.

Your voice.

Your laughter.

Your story.

You are not too much.

You are not behind.

You are not broken.

You are becoming.

And becoming sacred.

There will be days when you will feel like you're moving backwards. Days when old habits try to return. Days when your confidence feels small. Do not let those days fool you. Growth is not a straight line — it is a circle, a stretching, a returning to your own truth again and again.

Promise yourself this:

I will not give up on me.

Not when it's hard.

Not when I'm tired.

Not when I don't understand the "why" yet.

Not when others doubt me.

Not even when I doubt myself.

Because the version of you that you are growing into is worth the journey.

She is the healed one.

The confident one.

The grounded one.

The one who walks with purpose.

The one who knows her voice has weight and her presence has value.

Keep becoming her.

One choice.

One day.

One breath at a time.

So keep shining.

We need you.

And she — the woman you are becoming — is waiting for you with open arms.

Chapter 8

Written By Allison K. James – Frison

Daughter, the World Will Call Her Many Things I Call Her 'The Black Unicorn'

A Daughter from Newark: A Gift from God

Although I did not give birth to my daughter, she was the perfect gift from God to my husband and me. From the moment she came into our lives, I realized she was exactly what I had been missing. She arrived at a time when we needed her just as much as she needed us. Her presence filled our home with a renewed sense of joy and completeness.

Through her, I have learned that love has no boundaries. She taught me to love more deeply, extend grace even when it is difficult, and practice a level of patience I did not know I had. She reminds me daily that family is not just biology—it is God's design. And His timing? Always perfect.

Motherhood Redefined

People used to tell me—harshly and without compassion—that I would never be a mother. That I would never have the privilege of being called "Mommy."

Because of my past, they said I was disqualified. And for a long time, I believed them.

But God had another plan.

In November 2018, on National Adoption Day, we welcomed a beautiful 10-year-old girl named Rashanna into our hearts and our home. She was shy, full of curiosity, and struggling to love the skin she was in.

Her hair was thick like wool. She needed glasses and braces. She wore a size nine shoe and stood five feet tall—at just ten years old. She was uniquely made, but like many little Black girls, she did not know how beautiful she truly was.

The Power of Naming

When she became comfortable enough, I asked her if she had a nickname.

"Yes," she said.

"What is it?" I asked.

She whispered, "Blackey."

When I asked if she liked that name, she told me "No."

"Then why didn't you tell anyone you didn't like it?" I asked.

She shrugged. She did not know.

That day, I taught her something that I believe every young girl should know:

"You have the power to determine what name people call you. No one gets to define you but you."

That night, I gave her a new name, "WizHer.

She lit up.

"You know why I gave you that name?" I asked.

"Because I'm smart and I'm a girl!" she replied.

I asked, "Who's the smartest person in your classroom?"

She began naming others.

I stopped her and said, "No. You are."

Then I repeated the question.

"Who's the smartest person in your classroom?"

This time, she said it proudly: "I am!"

A New Path

She went from orphan to foster care to adopted.

From self-doubt to valedictorian of her graduation class.

From the schoolhouse into being the youngest politician in Newark, NJ.

From unseen to college graduate at 18.

Today, she is a junior at HBCU, studying criminal justice on a full scholarship.

Why? Because my husband and I were presents. We showed up for her education, her healing, her future.

A Word to Parents

Be mindful of the words you say over your children.

Never allow anyone, not even yourself, to call them anything less than who they truly are.

What It Means to Raise a Black Daughter

Raising a Black daughter means nurturing a young leader—one conversation, one affirmation, and one safe space at a time. It is a sacred calling that requires intention, strength, and deep love.

The world will try to tell her who she is—or worse, who she is not—before she even has a chance to define herself.

Representation is Power

Black girls often grow up without seeing themselves in leadership, on magazine covers, in textbooks, or celebrated in media. Instead, they are boxed into harmful stereotypes:

The angry Black girl

The oversexualized woman

The strong one who does not need help

These are dangerous lies.

They rob Black girls of vulnerability, innocence, and the right to just be.

School as the First Battleground

Research shows that Black girls are disciplined more harshly, labeled defiant, and judged unfairly. Their natural hair may be deemed "unprofessional." Their voices may be silent. The message? That who they are—naturally—is not acceptable.

As a parent, you must advocate early and often.

Let her know that her voice, her hair, and her brilliance are not only acceptable, but they are also sacred.

The Weight of Safety

The intersection of race and gender brings harsh realities:

Black and brown girls are at higher risk of trafficking, abuse, and police violence

Their stories often go untold or ignored

They are overpoliced, overexposed, and under protected

That is why we have the hard conversations early—about racism, consent, boundaries, and resilience. Not to instill fear, but to equip her with armor made of truth and awareness.

The Pressure of Social Media

In the digital age, popularity is currency, and image is everything.

Colorism runs deep.

Eurocentric beauty is still the standard.

But home must be her refuge.

Let your daughter know:

Her hair is a crown

Her skin is a blessing

Her voice is a gift

Her presence is power

Preparing Her to Lead

Raising a Black daughter is not just about shielding her. It is about preparing her.

Introduce her to the legacies of Black women who wrote, built, led, and thrived.

Teach her to walk in dignity—not because the world demands it, but because she deserves it.

Let her follow her passion even if they do not fit into the world's mold.

She Is Not a Burden

She is not the labels the world tries to stick on her.

She is not "too much" for any space.

The Book of Allison: The Wounds You Don't See

She is not defined by her trauma.

She is brilliant, beautiful, bold, and more than enough.

And Still, She Rises

Yes, there will be hard days.

She will ask questions that break your heart.

She will come home with wounds you cannot always fix.

But there will be joy.

There will be days when you watch her soar—despite the storm.

And in those moments, you will know:

The world may try to dim her light—but it can never extinguish it.

Author Rashanna E. James – Frison 'The Black Unicorn"

A Daughter from Newark: Book can be found on Amazon.

Follow her on IG: adaughterfromnewark

Facebook: Author Rashanna E. James Frison

Chapter 8 Workbook: The World Will Call Her Many Things: A Daughter from Newark

Scripture: Proverbs 22:6 KJV

Summary:

This chapter explores the deep struggles and hidden wounds tied to this theme. It invites you to reflect honestly and discover the truths hidden within our daughter's.

A Reflection Prompt:

What words have you spoken over your daughter, niece, goddaughter, or mentee? Are they building her up or breaking her down?

_____
_____
_____
_____
_____
_____
_____
_____
_____
_____
_____
_____
_____

A Legacy Challenge:

Write a letter to a young Black girl in your life. Remind her of who she is before the world tries to tell her otherwise.

Reflection Questions:

1. What labels have others given you?

_____
_____
_____
_____

2. Which of those labels do I accept, and which do I reject?

_____
_____
_____
_____

Affirmation:

"I am not my past. I am my strength."

Journal Space:

_____
_____
_____
_____
_____
_____
_____
_____
_____
_____
_____
_____

The Book of Allison: The Wounds You Don't See

A Prayer or Affirmation:

"God, help me to raise her with wisdom, to protect her with truth, and to empower her with love."

Chapter 9

Written By Allison K. James – Frison

Called to Serve, I Am Glad I Answered the Call

My experience planted something deep in me: a conviction that no family/child should be left without hope, support, or the chance to heal. So, when I made the decision to go to college, I had one goal in mind—become a social worker, not just any social worker, a social worker with Child Protective Services.

My dream was clear: to work with the Division of Child Protection and Permanency, not to separate families, but to help keep them together, if possible and safe. I wanted to be the person who showed up at the door not just with authority, but with resources, compassion, and a plan for rebuilding.

Every home I walk into reminds me of my own upbringing. I know what it feels like to live with uncertainty, to face struggles that others might not see, and to pray for a helping hand that does not judge but understands. That is why when I sit with families, I do not see "clients" or "cases." I see reflections of myself, my family, human beings, and my community.

My mission is simple but powerful: whatever obstacles a family is facing, I stay with them until we can find solutions. I pour my energy into making sure they walk away stronger than the day before. Sometimes it is connecting them to resources they did not know existed. Sometimes it is just sitting and listening when the world feels like it is against them. But always, it is about restoring hope.

The families I serve share pieces of my own story, the hardships, the struggles, the quiet resilience it takes to keep going. That is why I can sit across from them and say, "I understand." Not because of a textbook, but because I have lived it. And that shared understanding is what fuels my work.

Every morning, I wake up knowing that I have the chance to have influence in a family's life. I know that with the right tools, resources, and compassion, I can help shift their story from one of survival to one of thriving. I carry the memory of growing up in the Stella Wright Projects and my life's story.

They remind me of why I chose this path. And they remind me that my purpose as a social worker is not just to protect children, but to protect hope, to give families the opportunity to heal, and to fight for their right to stay together whenever it's safe and possible.

This is not just a career for me—it is a calling. It is a promise to show up, to listen, to guide, and to empower. It is a commitment to honor every child, every parent, and every family I encounter. It is knowing that the difference between despair and hope can be one person willing to stand in the gap.

I have learned that service is more than action: empathy in motion, love in practice, and faith in action. It is showing up even when it is hard, when there is no family support, when the weight of trauma or hopelessness threatens to overwhelm. Service is the light we carry into darkness, the voice that whispers to the weary, "You are not alone."

And so, I continue. I continue because of the children who deserve a chance, the families who deserve stability, and the communities that deserve healing. I continue because of my own journey—from trauma to triumph, from silence to voice, from despair to hope.

Every life I touch, every family I help, is a reminder that purpose is born from pain, and that even the smallest acts of care can create ripples of change far beyond what we can see.

I am a social worker. I am a mentor. I am a mother, a wife, and a leader. I am proof that one life, guided by compassion, resilience, and faith, can have influence. And if my story teaches anything, it is this: your purpose will find you, and when it does, when that phone rings, you better answer the call.

The Book of Allison: The Wounds You Don't See

Chapter 9 Workbook: Called to Serve – Guided Reflections & Exercises

Section 1: Understanding Your Calling

1. Reflective Journal Prompt

What does the word "calling" mean to you at this stage of your life?
_____
_____
_____
_____
_____

Have you ever felt pulled toward a purpose greater than yourself? Describe that moment.
_____
_____
_____
_____
_____
_____
_____

2. Self-Discovery Exercise – The Seed of Purpose

Your chapter speaks about a conviction being planted in you.

Complete the sentence:

"A seed was planted in me when…"
_____
_____
_____
_____
_____

"That moment taught me that my purpose might be…"_____
_____
_____
_____
_____
_____

3. Clarity Check

Rate on a scale of 1–10:

How connected do you feel to your life's purpose right now?

What would help you move one point higher?

_____
_____
_____
_____
_____
_____
_____
_____
_____

Section 2: Compassion in Action

5. Exercise – The Mirror Principle

Write down three qualities in yourself that help you connect with others on a deeper level:

1.

2.

3.

Then answer:

How can I use these qualities to show up more authentically in service?

_____
_____
_____
_____
_____
_____
_____

Section 3: Serving Through Lived Experience

6. Journaling Prompt – What I've Lived Makes Me Powerful

Your story teaches that lived experience gives empathy to its depth.

Reflect:

What part of your own journey allows you to understand others better?

How can you use that experience to guide someone today?

7. Reframing Exercise – Shame to Service to Strength

List three past hardships.

1. _____
2. _____
3. _____

Then rewrite each one as a strength or lesson it gave you.

1. _____
2. _____
3. _____

Hardship I Faced Strength or Wisdom, It Gave Me

Section 4: Holding Hope for Others

8. Prompt – Being the Light in Darkness

If You wrote, "Service is the light we carry into darkness."

Answer:

Who carried light for you when you were struggling?

How can you become that source of hope for someone else?

9. Activity – The Hope List

List five things you can offer someone who is feeling hopeless:

1.

2.

3.

4.

5.

Section 5: Empowering Families & Communities

10. Reflection – Seeing Strength in Struggle

Think about a time you helped someone.

What strengths did you see in them that they didn't recognize?

How did acknowledging those strengths change their situation?

11. Values Check – What You Stand On

Circle the values that guide your service:

Compassion — Service — Faith — Empathy — Resilience — Courage — Integrity — Hope — Patience — Advocacy — Justice — Understanding

Then write:

Why these values matter to me:

How these values show up in my daily life:

Section 6: Answering the Call

12. Prompt – Why I Show Up

Reflect on your purpose:

Why do I show up for others even when I'm tired?

What keeps me committed to my calling?

What message do I hope people receive from my presence?

13. Visualization Exercise – A Day in My Purpose

Close your eyes and imagine yourself five years from now walking fully in your calling.

Write down:

Where you are

Who you are helping

How your presence impacts them

How you feel serving in that moment

Section 7: Personal Declaration

14. Declaration of Purpose

Fill in the blanks to create your own calling statement:

"I am called to _____.

I serve with _____.

My life's purpose is to _____.

I will continue showing up because _____.

My story has taught me that _____."

The Book of Allison: The Wounds You Don't See

Section 8: Closing Reflection

15. Final Prompt – Answering the Call

Your chapter ends with:

"Your purpose will find you, and when it does, you better answer the call."

Reflect:

Did I answer my call—or am I still waiting?

What steps do I need to take this week to walk toward my purpose?

What promise am I making to myself today?

Chapter 10

Written By Allison K. James – Frison

My Second Chance: When the Dust Clears

When the World Said No — God Said Yes

The life of trauma took more from me than ever gave.

It claimed my silence, my tolerance, and my trust—only to leave me feeling empty.

But even in that emptiness, something unbreakable stirred. The wounds no one could see became the roots of a silent strength that kept me moving. I had to decide what was best for me—not just to survive, but to live.

I remember the first time I looked at myself in the mirror after it all—after sleeping in my van, after sharing beds with children who weren't mine, after the bruises, the empty bottles of alcohol, the death after death, the gun violence, the loneliness that sat so heavy on my chest I could barely breathe.

I almost did not recognize the woman staring back at me.

But in that imbalance, I learned the meaning of acceptance.

My eyes carried both the shadows of a thousand storms and the quiet fire of someone who had outlived them all. And in those ashes, fragments of grace remained—a light that began to shine on the woman I was becoming.

Second Chances Are Not Pretty

Second chances are not soft, gift-wrapped miracles.

They are forged in fire and fought for every single day.

Mine came through small, stubborn acts:

Waking up sober.

Holding the keys to my own place.

Choosing people who chose me back.

Saying "no" when my body had been trained to say "yes" out of fear.

Forgiving myself for the days I stumbled, for the moments I stayed silent when I should have spoken.

I have learned that survival is not the same as living.

Survival is keeping your head above water.

Living is learning to swim again feeling the sun on your face without bracing for another storm.

I gave myself permission to trust my journey and not fear what was ahead.

Today, my life is not perfect—but it is mine.

Built from rubble. Brick by brick. My second chance did not come all at once. It came in pieces—just like I did.

And as I put myself back together, I realized:

I am not who I was before the pain.

I am stronger.

Wiser.

Fiercer.

When the dust finally cleared, I was not the same woman.

I was better not bitter.

And that—despite everything—was worth surviving for.

I no longer beg for love that should be given freely.

Fear no longer holds me.

I live in the strength of my own power.

Scripture

Isaiah 43:18–19 (NIV)

"Forget the former things; do not dwell on the past.

See, I am doing a new thing!

Now it springs up; do you not perceive it?

I am making a way in the wilderness and streams in the wasteland."

The Other Side of Resilience

Homelessness taught me the raw definition of survival.

I walked the streets pretending I was fine while crumbling inside.

I learned that dignity does not come from what you own, it comes from holding on to yourself when the world tries to strip you bare.

The world had me dangling on the edge of a cliff—but God grabbed me and never let go.

And just when I thought my heart could not carry anymore, God sent someone to help carry it.

I call him Andre.

My Poppa Bear.

My silent hero.

And everything began to change.

The Chance Encounter: Becoming Allison K. James – Frison

Andre and I both went to Central High School but never crossed paths back then. I was a senior; he was a sophomore.

Who would have guessed that 25 years later, God would place us in the same place at the same time—on a class reunion cruise that neither of us was even supposed to attend?

I remember stepping onto the boat and hearing a man call out, "Hello!"

I quickly responded, "I'm not Zanna—I'm Allison." Remember everyone thought we were twins and could not tell us apart.

With a wide smile, he replied, "I know exactly who you are, Allison."

I brushed it off.

Later that night, after a few too many drinks, my favorite song came on, and I hit the dance floor. A man asked if he could join me. I said no. But when I turned around—there he was, dancing right behind me with that smile. At that time, I did not know he would be my future husband.

Something about his energy was genuine. When I sat down, he followed and asked for my number. I meant to give him a fake phone number—but in my intoxication state, I gave him the real one.

The next morning, I could not stop thinking about him.

Days passed, but no call came. Still, I could not get him off my mind.

Eventually, I found him through friends.

Once we reconnected... we never stopped dancing together, sixteen years later the drums are still beating.

A Love Rooted in Truth

On our first date, I told him everything:

The trauma. The violence. Alcoholism. The homelessness. The abuse.

I needed him to know what he was walking into.

He listened. No judgment.

Then he asked the one question no man had ever asked me:

"What are your plans for the future?" He did not care about the past; he was looking at how our future would be together.

Nervous, I answered:

"I want to start a nonprofit organization for girls."

He replied, without hesitation:

"Then what are you waiting for?"

We secretly dated for six months.

On my birthday in February 2009, the secret was out. He escorted me to my fortieth birthday party.

In September 2010, he proposed. We moved in together and began building something beautiful.

Through Sickness and Care

The day after Christmas 2011, I collapsed—numb on my left side.

Andre rushed me to the hospital. Diagnosis: a sciatic nerve issue.

For three months, he bathed me, fed me, brushed my hair, laid out my medicine, and kissed my forehead before work leaving me lunch and water at my nightstand.

When the pain was unbearable, he carried me to the ER—tired but unwavering.

By April, I was walking—with a limp.

By May, I collapsed again.

This time, it was worse.

I blacked out at work and landed in the ER in Bergen County.

Andre found me within minutes—carrying a plate of oxtails, my favorite.

Before my emergency surgery, he kissed my forehead—tears in his eyes.

The surgery was supposed to last three hours. It took twelve.

When I finally woke up, I called out his name over and over. The nurses told me he had called every hour asking for updates.

When I was wheeled into my room, there he was—smiling, whispering another kiss onto my forehead. I felt like I was sleeping beauty.

Two weeks later, I walked through the hospital's west wing—determined.

Pain or not, I was going to marry the man God sent to protect and love me unconditionally.

And I did.

On October 14, 2012, I became Allison K. James-Frison—wife to my best friend, Andre Frison

A Life Rebuilt

Since that day, we have honored every vow.

He has never hurt me, but he only held me.

He has never disrespected me—only uplifted me.

He calls me "baby" not BITCH.

Together we've:

Earned two degrees.

We purchased two homes.

Adopted a daughter.

Launched a nonprofit.

Stepped into politics.

Separately, Andre built businesses.

And I found the courage to put my story into this book. All because God placed us on that boat, that night, and changed everything, I was given a second chance.

Who I Was, Who I Am

Domestic violence left deep wounds—ones that whispered lies:

"You're not worth loving."

"No one will stay unless they hurt you."

But I have learned:

The hardest part was not leaving.

It was believing I deserved to.

My childhood was not a sanctuary. It was stolen—replaced with silence and shame.

Alcohol came next. A false friend.

It numbed the pain—until it controlled me.

Recovery was not just about quitting. It was about learning to sit with my pain without drowning in it.

And gun violence?

The Book of Allison: The Wounds You Don't See

It shattered me more than once.

There is no explaining the sound of a phone call that tells you someone is gone.

That pain lives inside me like folded letters I carry in my chest.

But still—here I am.

I am who I am because of everything I have walked through.

I am not ashamed of my past.

I am grateful for my healing.

I am not a victim—I am a victor.

And when the dust cleared…

I found me.

And, if I could do it, you could too.

Chapter 10 Workbook: When the World Said No: God Said Yes, My Second Chance Part 1

Scripture: Isaiah 43:18-19 NIV

Summary:

This chapter explores the deep struggles and hidden wounds tied to this theme. It invites you to reflect honestly and discover healing through faith, resilience, and the power of second chances.

Reflection Questions:

1. What doors closed in your past that felt permanent?

2. Where have you seen God create new opportunities for me?

Activity: Second Chance Roadmap

Draw or list steps you want to take toward your next chapter.

Affirmation:

"I am not my past. I am my strength."

The Book of Allison: The Wounds You Don't See

Journal Space:

The Book of Allison: The Wounds You Don't See

Chapter 10 Workbook: Second Chance: The Other Side of Broken – Resilience Part 2

Scripture: Genesis 2:24 NIV

Summary:

This chapter explores the deep struggles and hidden wounds tied to this theme. It invites you to reflect honestly and discover healing through faith, resilience, and the power of second chances.

Reflection Questions:

1. What does resilience mean to me personally?

2. How do I know I am stronger now than before?

Activity: Resilience Journal

Write about a moment when you thought you would break, but instead you grew stronger.

_____
_____
_____
_____
_____
_____
_____

Affirmation:

"I am not my past. I am my strength."

Journal Space:

The Book of Allison: The Wounds You Don't See

Chapter 11

Written By Allison K. James – Frison

Spiritual Encounters: The Blessing I Needed to See

There are moments in life when the veil between this world and the next becomes thin. Moments when the people we've lost, the angels assigned to us, or the signs meant for us breakthrough in ways we can't explain. These encounters aren't coincidences — they are reminders. Reminders that we are seen, guided, and loved, even when we feel alone. In this chapter, I share some of the spiritual encounters that shaped my journey, restored my faith, and brought healing to places I didn't even know were wounded.

The Ride I Didn't Expect

I remember that morning like it happened yesterday. I was running on routine, moving on autopilot the way you do when life keeps you busy and tired at the same time. I climbed onto the bus headed to work, expecting nothing more than another loud ride. Normally, I go straight to the back. That's my spot — because I am always one of the ones to get off the bus last at the last stop.

But that morning, something nudged me to sit up front. To this day I can't explain it. I just moved without thinking, as if something—someone—guided me.

The moment I sat down and glanced across the aisle, the air shifted. My breath caught in my throat. Sitting right there, just a few feet away, was my mother.

Not a memory.

Not a dream.

Not a resemblance.

My mother.

She was dressed exactly the way she always loved: her favorite trench coat, even though it was a hot summer day; that deep purple turban wrapped around her head; and her signature lipstick that she never left the house without. The same turban I wear now, without even thinking about why—maybe trying to stay connected to her all this time.

I froze. My whole body went still. She didn't speak, not one word. She just looked at me with this soft, knowing smile that felt like it reached right inside my chest. A smile only a mother can give. A smile I hadn't seen in years.

We locked eyes the entire ride. I swear I didn't blink once. I was afraid that if I looked away—even for a second—she would vanish. Every time the bus slowed down or stopped, I braced myself, waiting for her image to fade or for the woman I was seeing to get off. But she stayed. Stop after stop, she stayed.

Forty-five minutes.

Forty-five long minutes of her looking at me like she never left me at all.

I didn't know whether to cry, smile, or reach for her. I just sat there, suspended between disbelief and gratitude, feeling something holy in that moment. A peace I hadn't felt in years settled over me. It was as if she came to remind me that I wasn't walking through life alone, no matter how heavy things felt.

When we reached the last stop—my stop—I stood up slowly. My legs felt weak. Before stepping off the bus, I turned around one more time, almost afraid to look, but needing to. Wanting to hold on to her face for just one more second.

But she was gone.

The seat was empty.

As if she'd never been there at all.

Yet I knew what I saw. I knew what I felt. Some moments can't be explained, only experienced. That morning wasn't just a bus ride to work — it was a visit, a reminder, a whisper from the other side. A spiritual encounter wrapped in an ordinary moment.

#Dear God #Thank You #Spiritual Encounter

The Visitor Meant for Me

Andre had been praying for months to see his guardian angel. Every night before bed, every quiet moment before work, every time he felt discouraged, he asked God for just one sign — one glimpse of the divine watching over him. I knew how much it meant to him. It became part of the rhythm of our home: his hope, his waiting, his faith stretching toward heaven.

Then one morning, something happened that neither of us expected.

I was still half-asleep when I heard a soft voice say, "Hello." It wasn't loud, but it was clear — gentle, almost magical. Andre, without even fully waking up, mumbled back, "Hey," as if the voice belonged to someone familiar. I thought it was our daughter, who might have come into the room because she needed something. So I lifted my head to check on her.

But instead of my child, I saw a bright figure.

It wasn't like anything I had ever seen before — bright lights, peaceful, almost glowing from the inside. The light wasn't harsh; it felt warm, comforting, like it carried a presence I couldn't put into words. The figure smiled at me with such kindness, and again said, "Hello." And then, just as quickly as it appeared, it faded away right in front of me.

I sat up fully awake this time, heart racing, unsure whether to be afraid or grateful. I shook Andre gently and told him what had just happened — every detail, every word, every second.

He sat up too, but his face fell. Months of praying, waiting, hoping… yet the moment he longed for was given to me instead. I understood his disappointment. I felt it with him. It didn't feel fair.

Later that morning, we called our Family Deacon, Deacon Daniels — the one assigned to our household through the church we attended at the time. I told him everything, from the voice to the bright figure to Andre's hurt over missing the encounter he had prayed so hard for.

The Deacon listened quietly and then said something simple, but powerful:

"The person who had the encounter was the one who was meant to see it."

Those words sank into me. I didn't know why I was chosen in that moment, or why Andre's prayer was answered through my eyes instead of his. But I knew the experience was real, intentional, and meant for me — even if part of me wished it had been given to him.

Sometimes God responds in ways we don't expect. And sometimes the message isn't just for the one who prays — but for the one who witnesses.

#DearGod #ThankYou #SpiritualEncounter

The White Deer on the Parkway

A few days after my adopted daughter's biological mother passed away, I found myself on the Garden State Parkway, lost in heavy traffic and heavier thoughts. I kept thinking about Rashanna's mother, Keisha. My heart was unsettled.

At that time, I wanted Rashanna to come live with me, but after the homegoing service, my sister and niece went back and forth, both saying they wanted her. I didn't want to be part of that tug-of-war. As long as she was with family, I told myself I would be at peace. But deep down, I wasn't.

The traffic that day was bumper to bumper. Cars as far as I could see. But then something strange happened — the cars began to thin out, almost as if they simply disappeared. I ended up on a stretch of road with no one in front of me and no one behind me.

And then it appeared.

A snow-white deer stepped out onto the parkway.

I slammed on my brakes so hard my whole body jerked forward. My first thought was: Lord, don't let me hit this animal. My second thought was to check my rearview mirror to brace for someone crashing into the back of me. But when I looked, there were no cars. Not one. Just empty road.

I turned my eyes forward again, and the deer was standing there, perfectly still. We locked eyes — me and this pure, white creature that looked like it stepped out of a dream. It held my gaze for several long seconds, calm, unbothered, almost knowing. Then it slowly crossed the parkway and disappeared into the trees like it was never there.

I didn't have to guess what the message was.

All I said out loud was, "Keisha heard my heart. I understood. She knows where she wants her daughter to be."

Six years passed before that message became real. Six years before Rashanna walked into our home for good. By then, Andre and I had just purchased our first house — three bedrooms, already painted one blue and the other purple. Colors waiting on a child we didn't even know would be ours.

I couldn't have children of my own, and one day I looked at Andre and said, "God is going to bless us with children. I don't know how, but it's going to happen." We both laughed, not knowing the truth of what I'd just spoken.

Then the phone call came.

We were walking out the door, bags packed for vacation, when someone from Child Protection Services, her case worker, asked if we wanted Rashanna to come stay with us. "Yes," we said immediately. "When is she coming?"

"Today," they responded.

I asked if she could come next week so we could prepare properly, once we return from our vacation, and the voice on the phone said, "It's today… or no day."

That was all we needed to hear. We canceled our trip on the spot.

God's timing, not ours.

It was a test — one final sign — to see what mattered most: a vacation or the child we had prayed for, the child God had already chosen for us years earlier on that empty stretch of the Garden State Parkway.

America, pay attention to the signs. Don't just focus on the message – the lesson is the most important part of the blessing. They don't always come the way you expect. But they always come right on time.

#DearGod #ThankYou #SpiritualEncounter

The Night My Nephew Passed By

When my nephew passed away, grief wasn't the only weight I carried. Soon after his death, family rumors started circulating — whispers that he had been mad at me before he died. I couldn't understand it. Every time he called, I answered. Anytime he needed me, I showed up. Why would anyone say that? Why would they wait until he was gone to put that kind of pain on my heart? The rumor tore me apart. I cried through therapy sessions, trying to make sense of why people who knew how close we were would speak something so cruel and so untrue. Grief is already heavy, but the idea that my nephew left this world upset with me felt unbearable.

A few weeks after his homegoing service, something happened that lifted a burden I didn't even know how to release.

I was at a hotel. I woke up in the middle of the night to use the bathroom. Still half asleep, I put one foot on the floor — and when I looked up, there he was, my nephew walked right past me.

He wasn't a shadow or a blur. He was clear. Solid. Familiar.

He had on his favorite blue and black hoodie, a pair of jeans, and in his hand, he carried a black garbage bag — I assumed his belongings were in it. He didn't look at me. He didn't slow down. He was just walking upward, as if following a path only he could see.

I remember whispering to myself, "He's on his way to heaven."

I never saw his face — only the back of him — but I felt peace instead of fear. I was smiling and crying at the same time.

When I finally gathered myself, I went straight to my phone and sent a group message to my siblings, to his siblings, and to other close family members. I told them exactly what I saw. I even shared it on social media. The first thing everyone asked was, "Why didn't he come to my house?" or "Why didn't he stop to see me?"

All I said was, "Maybe he's making his rounds."

But as soon as the words left my mouth, I remembered what my Family Deacon had once told me after a different spiritual encounter:

"The person who had the experience was the one who was meant to see it."

And at that moment, I understood.

My nephew wasn't mad at me.

He wasn't carrying bitterness.

He wasn't holding anything against me.

He came through to show me that.

That quiet moment in the dark — him walking upward, moving forward, at peace — lifted a heavy weight off my heart. It was his way of telling me that love was still intact, and the rumors were nothing but noise.

Sometimes healing comes in ways we can't explain. And sometimes the people we love don't need to say a word for us to finally understand.

#DearGod #ThankYou #SpiritualEncounter

Chapter 11 Workbook: Spiritual Encounters

A Guided Journal for Reflection, Healing & Understanding

Introduction

Spiritual encounters often arrive during moments of pain, transition, or deep reflection. These moments are personal, powerful, and sometimes confusing. This workbook helps readers slow down, process their experiences, and uncover the messages, comfort, or guidance meant for them.

Each section guides the reader through:

Understanding the encounter

Naming their emotions

Identifying the message

Connecting it to their healing journey

The Book of Allison: The Wounds You Don't See

Section 1: Preparing Your Heart

1. What is a Spiritual Encounter to You?

Write what you personally believe spiritual encounters are and how you interpret them.

Reflection:

_____
_____
_____
_____
_____
_____
_____
_____
_____

2. How Do You Usually Sense the Spiritual?

(Check all that apply)

☐ Dreams

☐ Visions

☐ Signs in nature

☐ Voices or whispers

☐ Strong intuition

☐ Feelings or chills

☐ Repeating numbers

☐ Unexpected peace

Describe your typical experiences:

Section 2: Documenting a Spiritual Encounter

Use this section each time you have an encounter.

Encounter Log #1

1. Date & Time _____

2. Location _____

Where were you when it happened?
_____

The Book of Allison: The Wounds You Don't See

3. What Happened?

Describe everything you saw, heard, felt, or sensed. Don't filter.

_____
_____
_____
_____
_____
_____
_____
_____
_____
_____
_____
_____
_____
_____
_____
_____

_____

4. Emotions You Felt

(Check any that apply)

☐ Peace

☐ Fear

☐ Confusion

☐ Comfort

☐ Love

☐ Sadness

☐ Joy

☐ Relief

☐ Other: _____

5. What Did You Think This Meant in the Moment?

6. What Message Do You Believe Was Being Given to You?

7. Did This Encounter Bring You Healing?

☐ Yes

☐ No

☐ Not sure yet

Explain:

Section 3: Understanding Signs & Symbols

1. Symbol Interpretation

List any symbols you saw (animals, colors, numbers, objects, people) and what they mean to you.

_____
_____
_____
_____
_____

Symbol: What It Represents to You: How It Connects to Your Life

2. Repeated Signs

Have you seen this symbol before?

_____
_____
_____
_____

Section 4: Emotions & Healing

1. What Comfort Did You Feel?

_____
_____
_____
_____

2. What Part of Yourself Needed This Moment?

_____
_____
_____
_____

3. What Healing Action Can You Take Next?

(Prayer, therapy, journaling, forgiveness, rest, boundaries, etc.)

_____
_____
_____
_____

Section 5: Messages From Loved Ones

1. Who Do You Believe Visited or Spoke to You?

2. What Was Unfinished or Unsaid Between You?

3. Did This Encounter Bring Closure or Clarity? How?

Section 6: Strengthening Your Spiritual Awareness

Daily Practices

Morning gratitude

Evening reflection

Prayer or meditation

Quiet time

Nature walks

Keeping a journal

Paying attention to patterns

Listening to your intuition

Your Personal Commitment

Write one promise to yourself that will help you notice spiritual moments more clearly.

_____
_____
_____
_____
_____
_____
_____
_____
_____
_____
_____

Section 7: Additional Encounter Logs

(Repeat the following pages for readers to document multiple experiences.)

Encounter #2

(Use same questions as Encounter #1)

Encounter #3

Encounter #4

Encounter #5

Section 8: Closing Reflection

1. After completing this workbook, how have your beliefs shifted?

_____
_____
_____
_____
_____
_____
_____

2. What have you learned about yourself?

_____
_____
_____
_____

3. What messages or signs feel the most meaningful to your journey right now?

Closing Chapter

As you turn these pages and leave this chapter behind, I pray you carry one truth with you: the spiritual world is not far from us. It shows up in the quiet, in the unexpected, and in the moments, we need it the most. My encounters were never about fear — they were about reassurance. They reminded me that I am guided, protected, and watched over, even when life feels overwhelming.

If you have ever questioned your own signs or brushed off a moment that felt too real to ignore, I encourage you to pay closer attention. Healing doesn't always arrive in the ways we imagine. Sometimes it comes through the unseen. Sometimes it comes through the ones we've lost. And sometimes, it comes simply to tell us we are not alone.

#DearGod #ThankYou #IWasNeverAlone

'Hold The Pen' Your Roadmap to Authorship.

From vision to victory. From pen to paper. From paper to published. From author to authorship.

This is your sign: Stop sitting on the book inside you. Your story deserves a cover, a title, and a place on someone's bookshelf. I'm coaching new authors through every step of the journey — idea, writing, publishing, and beyond.

Closing Reflection

My journey has been long, winding, and at times unbearably heavy. From the streets of Newark to the halls of education, from the silence of trauma to the light of healing, from moments of despair to the joy of family and purpose—every chapter of my life has shaped the person I am today.

I share these stories not for sympathy, but for truth. Not to dwell on pain, but to show resilience. Not to highlight struggles, but to illuminate hope. Your past does not define you; it can refine you. Your wounds do not disqualify you; they can guide you. Every tear, every setback, every silence, can become fuel for strength, courage, and compassion.

I have learned that life is not about perfection, it is about persistence. It is about standing up again when the world has knocked you down, about claiming your worth when others try to deny it and about using your experiences to lift others as you rise. My story is proof that no matter how dark the night the dawn will come. No matter how heavy the burden, hope can carry you forward. To every reader holding this book, know this: your voice matters, your story matters, and your dreams matter. God has placed you here for a reason, with a purpose uniquely yours.

Trust the journey, embrace the lessons, and walk boldly in the life you were created to lead.

You are not defined by what happened to you, but by what you choose to do with it. You are not broken, you are becoming. You are not alone, and you are deeply loved.

Go into the world with faith, courage, and compassion. Live fully. Love fiercely. Laugh often. And shine your light because the world needs your story, your voice, and your brilliance. Now go into your next chapter with confidence, and with your eyes wide open.

May peace be with you,

Author Allison K. James – Frison

ABOUT THE AUTHOR

Allison is an overcomer and reflects the true persevering spirit of resilience. Like many girls born in urban communities, Allison was not a child born of means, privilege, or access. She was raised in subsidized housing in the city of Newark, NJ Stella Wright Projects; an environment that presented its own unique set of life challenges. At an early age Allison lost both of her parents, experienced and survived domestic violence, gun violence, child sexual abuse, and homelessness.

Despite life's hard knocks, she used these adversities as fuel for her fire to be and do more! Each traumatic experience served as a unique catalyst for her aspiration to create something larger than herself. Allison felt that during her childhood she was deprived of opportunities to live, love, and laugh. She vowed to one day create an organization that would fill the void for girls in the community who may have had similar experiences.

Allison is a woman of action and true to her word. In 2009, she founded Girls; Live, Love, Inc. (GLLL).

Girls Live, Love, Laugh Inc. is a 501c (3) nonprofit organization focusing on scholars living with limited resources in the inner city of Newark, New Jersey. The organization builds a safe passage for building leadership skills, developing self-esteem, entrepreneurship, acquiring college readiness skills, the fundamentals of savings, and teaching the importance of civic engagement in the community. GLLL implements a variety of programs that focus on tackling many of the pressing issues girls face today. GLLL is building a culture of girls who live, love, and laugh while in pursuit of excellence.

Allison has built a foundation from the same Newark soil that once deprived her of her childhood she found her deepest passion to give girls an opportunity to develop in a healthy environment, after she rose from the ashes of personal struggles to date Allison's organization has mentored over two-thousand girls with an 89% track record of girls attending college.

Allison and her organization Girls: Live, Love, Laugh Inc. are the first to receive esteem recognition in Newark, NJ. However, what Allison is most proud of is obtaining an associate degree from Essex County College (with honors) and Rutgers University- Newark at the age of fifty-years old making her a first generation graduate out of seven siblings. Her associate's degree from Essex County College would be the spark that led to more educational opportunities.

Allison is an Investigator for the Department of Child Protection and Permanency, the Vice President at Newark Board of Education serving over 44,000 students, an active member of Pleasant Grove Cathedral. Allison also served as a Commissioner on the Status of Women in Newark, New Jersey, and is a Chartering Member of National Council of Negro Women: Greater Essex County Area Section.

Besides being a community servant, Allison is a loving wife, mother, and a member of Alpha Kappa Alpha Sorority Incorporated and Gamma Phi Delta Sorority, Incorporated.

Allison has received the recognitions below and has been honored throughout the city, county, and state: Every resolution, every honor, every act of kindness has help shape me and realize that my story was a part of God's glory for me.

- Senate Resolution – Women's History Month 2025
- Pleasant Grove Baptist Church Community Activist Award 2025

- Greater Friendship Baptist Church Women's Ministry: Community & Kingdom Building Award – 2024
- McKinley School Newark, NJ International Women's Day Award - 2024
- 211 W.I.M. Community Service and Philanthropy Award – 2022
- Senate and General Assembly Citation: A woman of creator, determination, and enterprise – 2022
- Vashi School of Future Leaders Humanitarian Award – 2019
- Women Initiative Self-Empowerment Organization – Outstanding Leadership Award – 2019
- Rutgers University – Newark Women's History Month Stirring Committee – No More Hidden Figures "The SHEheros Amongst Us. – 2018
- Mayor Ras J. Baraka City of Newark Proclamation which declared September 14th as 'Allison James – Frison Day' - 2018
- Essex County Board of Chosen Freeholder – Resolution for Girls Empowerment – 2018
- The State and General Assembly Joint Legislative – Resolution for Leadership 2018
- Bennett College Northern New Jersey Alumni Associates - Black Girl Magic Award 2018
- Rutgers University Newark Appreciation for Outstanding Service Award by Social Work Dept. 2017& 2018
- Unified Vailsburg Services Organization – Community Service Award 2017
- Prudential Center & New Jersey Devil Newark's Cornerstone Finalist 2017
- Newark Mentoring Movement – Movement in Newark Future Youth Award 2017

- Horizon - Win, Rock, Rule Women Empowerment LeadHER Award 2017
- The State of New Jersey Senate Resolution Honoree by Senator Rice 2017
- The City of Newark, NJ Municipal Council Resolution Honoree by Councilwomen Gayle Chaneyfield Jenkins 2016
- Mount Pleasant Missionary Baptist Church – Women Empowerment Award 2016
- Newark Circle of Sister – Mentorship Award 2015
- New Vision Tabernacle CME Church WOW Ministry - Women in Ministry Award 2015
- Mount Pleasant Missionary Baptist Church - Mission Outreach Community Award 2014
- Newark Mayor Ras. Baraka –Girls; Live, Love, Laugh Inc. Proclamation 2014
- Central High School Alumni Associates - Merit for Mentorship & Community Service Award 2013

Resources:

Youth Leadership and Mentor Programs

Girls Live, Love, Laugh Inc.: girlslivelovelaugh.org

Therapist

Kadian Peynado

Epiphany Relationship and Family Counseling, LLC

Website: www.epiphrfc.com Email: Epiphrfc@gmail.com
Phone: 908 531 6905

Trauma & Child Abuse

National Child Abuse Hotline (Child help): 1-800-422-4453 (24/7 confidential support)

RAINN (Rape, Abuse & Incest National Network): 1-800-656-HOPE (4673) | online chat: online.rainn.org

National Domestic Violence Hotline: 1-800-799-SAFE (7233) | thehotline.org

Loveisrespect: 1-866-331-9474 | text "LOVEIS" to 22522 | loveisrespect.org

Homelessness: National Alliance to End Homelessness: 202-638-1526 | endhomelessness.org

HUD Homeless Assistance: 1-800-569-4287 | hud.gov

Local shelters and food banks: Check your city/county social services directory for programs near you.

Mental Health & Counseling

Substance Abuse and Mental Health Services Administration (SAMHSA) Helpline: 1-800-662-HELP (4357)

National Suicide Prevention Lifeline: 988 (24/7 confidential support) | suicidepreventionlifeline.org

Therapy Assistance Online Directory: psychologytoday.com

Domestic Violence & Safety

National Domestic Violence Hotline: 1-800-799-SAFE (7233) | text "START" to 88788

Safe Horizon (for victims of abuse, children, and families): 1-800-621-HOPE (4673) | safehorizon.org

Education & Learning Support

Learning Disabilities Association of America: 1-866-455-3272 | ldaamerica.org

National Center for Learning Disabilities: ncld.org

Your local school district special education office: Provides assessments, Individualized Education Plans (IEPs), and accommodations.

Adoption & Family Support

Adoption Network Cleveland: 216-325-1370 | adoptionnetwork.com

National Foster Care & Adoption Directory: childwelfare.gov/topics/adoption

National Parent Helpline: 1-855-427-2736 | nationalparenthelpline.org

Faith-Based Support

Local church or faith-based counseling centers can provide spiritual guidance, mentorship, and community programs.

New International Version and King James Version

Some of Allison's Favorite Bible verses for encouragement

Romans 8:18 NIV – "I consider that our present sufferings are not worth comparing with the glory that will be revealed in us."

Isaiah 43:18-19 NIV – "Forget the former things; do not dwell on the past. See, I am doing a new thing!"

Proverbs 1:7 NIV – "The fear of the LORD is the beginning of knowledge, but fools despise wisdom and instruction."

Proverbs 22:6 KJV – "Train up a child in the way he should go: And when he is old, he will not depart from it."

www.ingramcontent.com/pod-product-compliance
Lightning Source LLC
Chambersburg PA
CBHW071202160426
43196CB00011B/2164